Features dishes seen in ✪ *Crash Landing on You* ✪ *Hospital Playlist* ✪ *It's Okay to Not Be Okay*

THE
KOREAN
K-DRAMA
COOKBOOK

Make the Dishes Seen in
Your Favorite TV Shows!

Choi Heejae

TUTTLE Publishing

Tokyo | Rutland, Vermont | Singapore

Contents

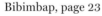

Bibimbap, page 23

Spicy Stir-fried Pork, page 39

Kimbap Sushi Rolls, page 73

Make the Dishes Seen in Your Favorite K-dramas!

Hello, I'm Choi Heejae. I've always been interested in food—I studied at Hattori Nutrition College in Tokyo and also at the Institute of Korean Royal Cuisine in Seoul. Now I run my own restaurant and cooking school in Seoul.

Recently, as Korean pop culture has spread around the world, my friends in other countries started saying that they loved watching K-dramas on TV and some of them had even tried making some of the Korean dishes they'd seen being eaten on these shows. That gave me the idea for writing this book. The recipes you'll find here aren't exactly the same as the ones you've seen in your favorite dramas—they are my original takes on those dishes. But I guarantee they are delicious!

Korean cooking uses a lot of vegetables and is very healthy—not only will you not get tired of it, you'll start craving it! It's also becoming a lot easier to get hold of Korean ingredients these days, either at your local Korean or Asian market, or online.

I hope that by making and eating the dishes in this book you'll not only deepen your enjoyment of your favorite K-dramas, but you'll feel a closer connection to my home country, Korea.

—Choi Heejae

Glossary of Korean Ingredients

You should be able to find these ingredients in your local Korean grocery store or Asian market. Wherever possible, recipes in this book offer substitute ingredients for Korean ingredients that may be hard to find.

Anchovies, dried
Called mareun-myeolchi in Korean, you can find these dried anchovies sold in packets in Korean groceries or in general Asian markets. The anchovies vary in size: the small ones are good for the recipes in this book.

Anchovy powder
Available in Korean grocery stores. If you can't find it, grind dried anchovies in a food processor.

Cheongju
Korean rice wine, clear in color, similar to Japanese sake. Sake can also be used for recipes in this book that call for cheongju.

Chrysanthemum greens
Called ssukgat in Korean, these have a distinctive grassy flavor. Use mustard greens or spinach as a substitute.

Chunjang black bean paste
A salty paste made of fermented soybeans and caramel, which gives it its color. It can be substituted with tianmian (Chinese fermented sweet bean sauce)

Corn syrup see Light corn syrup page 106

Daikon radish
A thick white root vegetable with a spicy flavor and a crunchy texture when raw. When cooked, it becomes soft and sweet. Widely available in Asian markets and also in many regular supermarkets.

Daikon radish, pickled
Noticeable for its yellow color, this pickled version of daikon radish, called danmuji in Korean can be bought readymade at Asian grocery stores. The Japanese version is called takuan and can also be used for the recipes in this book.

Dangmyeon noodles see page 106

Danmuji see Daikon radish, pickled

Chinese yam
A long root vegetable with pale brown skin and a viscous, slippery texture. You can find it at Chinese, Korean and Japanese grocery stores.

Dadaegi
A spicy sesame chili sauce (sometimes written as tategi in English), used to flavor a wide range of dishes. You can make your own meaty version following the recipe on page 115.

Dasima seaweed
Dried kelp, used as the basis for stock in many Korean recipes. Japanese kombu seaweed can also be used in recipes that call for dasima.

Doenjang
Doenjang is a type of soybean paste, similar to Japanese miso paste, and it is an indispensable ingredient in Korean cuisine. The soybeans are crushed roughly so that the texture of the beans is still evident, and it has a unique pungent aroma. Unlike Japanese miso, which can be ruined by cooking at too high a temperature for too long, the flavor of doenjang becomes more pronounced the longer it's cooked.

Fish cake
The type of fish cake used in this book is called eomuk in Korean, and is sold readymade in various shapes. The flat sheets will work well for the recipes in this book.

Gim seaweed
Gim seaweed is sold as dried flat sheets and is similar to Japanese nori seaweed, which can also be used in the recipes in this book.

Gochujang paste
This red chili paste is made by combining medium grain rice, short grain rice, rice koji, and red chili powder and fermenting it. It is spicy but also sweet and rich, and is served with bibimbap, and added to hot pots and other dishes.

Grated garlic
Grated or finely minced garlic is an indispensable ingredient in Korean cooking. You can use fresh garlic for any of the recipes in this book that call for grated garlic, but you can buy ready-grated or ready-minced garlic at Korean or general Asian grocery stores, which is convenient. Compared to regular garlic, the Korean variety is very aromatic and deep in flavor.

Green plum extract see page 32

Kalguksu noodles
Made from wheat flour and egg, these are sold dried in Korean or general Asian grocery stores.

Makgeolli
A slightly sparkling rice wine with a milky-white color.

Maesil-cheong see Green plum extract page 32

Mandu dumpling skins
Made of wheat flour and water, these can be bought readymade. Japanese gyoza skins can also be used for the recipes in this book.

Mareun-myeolchi see Anchovies, dried

Mirim
This is a sweet alcoholic liquor made from rice, and is used almost exclusively for cooking. It can be found in most Asian markets. The Japanese equivalent is called mirin and can also be used for recipes in this book.

Miyeok seaweed
This seaweed is sold dried at Korean and general Asian grocery stores. It is the same as Japanese wakame seaweed, which can also be used in the recipes in this book that call for miyeok.

Myeolchi-jeot see Salted anchovy extract page 32

Naengmyeon noodles see page 106

Perilla leaves
Don't confuse Korean perilla leaves (kkae) with Japanese perilla leaves (shiso). Although they look similar, kkae has an aniseed-like flavor and fragrance. Kkae has leaves with scalloped edges and purple-tinged undersides, whereas shiso leaves are lighter green with spiky edges.

Perilla oil see page 106

Ramyeon noodles
These are the equivalent of instant Japanese ramen noodles, sold in packets in Korean groceries or Asian markets.

Rice cakes see page 106

Rice vinegar
You can find Korean rice vinegar in your Korean grocery store. Japanese rice vinegar may be easier to find and can also be used in the recipes in this book, although Korean rice vinegar tends to be milder.

Salted anchovy extract see page 32

Salted pollack roe
This is a popular ingredient in Korea and Japan and can be found at well-stocked Asian grocery stores, often sold frozen. Its Korean name is myeongnan-jeot and its Japanese name is mentaiko.

Salted shrimp see page 32

Sesame oil
Dark sesame oil is essential in Korean dishes. In Korea it is used as a seasoning rather than as a cooking oil. Korean sesame oil has a dark color and is highly aromatic.

Shiitake mushrooms
Both dried and fresh shiitake mushrooms are used in the recipes in this book. They can be found in Japanese grocers and general Asian markets.

Shimeji mushrooms
Also known as beech mushrooms, these can be found in Asian markets.

Soju
A distilled alcoholic beverage that is clear and colorless and contains 20–24 percent alcohol by volume.

Somyeon noodles
Thin, wheat-flour noodles, often served cold. They are the same as Japanese somen noodles.

Squid, dried
Shredded dried squid is enjoyed as a snack in Korea and Japan and you can find it sold in packets in Asian markets.

Tempura flour
Combines wheat flour, starch, egg powder and baking powder, to allow you to make a batter for deep-frying easily. Widely available from general non-Asian supermarkets.

Tteok see Rice cakes page 106

Water celery
This Asian leafy vegetable is also known as Chinese celery, water dropwort or Japanese parsley. If you can't find it, try a mix of watercress and celery leaves as a substitute.

Wood ear mushrooms
Native to China, this black fungus can be bought dried in packets from Asian markets.

Yuja tea
A kind of jelly or jam sold in jars. Also called citron tea.

The K-dramas Featured in This Book

Crash Landing on You

A love story between an heiress who crash lands in North Korea in a paragliding accident and the army officer who hides her, and then falls in love with her.

Original air dates in South Korea: December 14, 2019–February 16, 2020 (19 episodes) **Cast:** Son Ye-jin (Yoon Se-ri), Hyun Bin (Lee Jeong-hyeok)

One Spring Night

One day, librarian Jung-in has a chance encounter with pharmacist and single father Ji Ho. They find they have many things in common, and they start to grow closer.

Original air dates in South Korea: May 22–July 11, 2019 (32 episodes) **Cast:** Han Ji-min (Lee Jung-in), Jung Hae-In (Yoo Ji Ho)

Itaewon Class

Sae Ro Yi's father was killed in an accident caused by the son of the chairman of the Jangga Group. Sae Ro Yi opens a restaurant in Seoul's Itaewon district and fights to make a go of it.

Original air dates in South Korea: January 31–March 21, 2020 (16 episodes) **Cast:** Park Seo-joon (Park Sae Ro Yi), Kim Da-Mi (Jo Yi Seo)

Hospital Playlist

Written by Woo-jung Lee, who is renowned amongst K-drama fans. A drama that focuses on five young doctors from the same class at Seoul University Medical School, now working at the same hospital.

Original air dates in South Korea: March 12–May 28, 2020 (25 episodes) **Cast:** Jo Jung-Suk (Lee Ik Joon), Jeon Mi Do (Chae Song Hwa)

She Was Pretty

Once a high-achieving beauty, Hye-jin is now unemployed and unattractive. Once a fat kid, Sung-joon now has flawless good looks. Two people who have traveled opposite routes in life fall in love.

Original air dates in South Korea: September 16–November 11, 2015 (16 episodes) **Cast:** Hwang Jeong-eum (Kim Hye-jin), Park Seo-joon (Ji Sung-joon)

What's Wrong With Secretary Kim?

The story of the romance between the rich, handsome, flawless second-generation heir to a fortune Young Joon, and Kim Mi So, the secretary who has supported him impeccably.

Original air dates in South Korea: June 6–July 26, 2018 (16 episodes) **Cast:** Park Seo-joon (Lee Young Joon), Park Min-Young (Kim Mi So)

It's Okay to Not Be Okay

A love story following the relationship between Gang Tae, a caretaker at a psychiatric ward, and Moon Young, a writer of children's books who does not know what love is—and how they heal each other's wounds.

Original air dates in South Korea: June 20 - August 9, 2020 (16 episodes) **Cast:** Kim Soo-hyun (Moon Gang Tae), Seo Ye-Ji (Go Moon Young)

The King: Eternal Monarch

Lee Gon, the modern-day Emperor of the Kingdom of Korea, attempts to close the gate to an alternative reality; female detective Tae Eul crosses between the two worlds while she attempts to preserve their love.

Original air dates in South Korea: April 17 - June 12, 2020 (16 episodes) **Cast:** Lee Min-Ho (Lee Gon), Kim Go-eun (Jeong Tae Eul)

Mystic Pop-up Bar

Based on a popular web comic. A fantasy drama where the beautiful woman owner and an innocent part-time employee of a mysterious outdoor bar visit their customers in their dreams and help to resolve their regrets and their grudges.

Original air dates in South Korea: May 20 - June 25, 2020 **Cast:** Hwang Jeong-eum (Weol Joo), Sung-Jae Yook (Han Kang Bae), Choi Wonyoung (Chief Gwi)

Familiar Wife

Unremarkable bank employee Joo-hyuk is berated by his wife Woo jin every day. Then one day, his first love appears, prompting him to make a decision that will catapult him into a totally different life.

Original air dates in South Korea: August 1–September 20, 2018 (16 episodes) **Cast:** Seong Ji (Cha Joo-hyuk), Han Ji-min (Seo Woo-jin)

Start-Up

A drama that depicts the lives of the young people who dream of success in South Korea's fictional Silicon Valley, Sandbox. The story changes course because of a lie by a grandmother who is thinking of her grandchild.

Original air dates in South Korea: October 17–December 6, 2020 (16 episodes) **Cast:** Kim Seon-Ho (Han Ji Pyung), Nam Joo-hyuk (Nam Do San)

Record of Youth

Set in the entertainment industry, this drama depicts the struggles of a young man who dreams of making the transition from modeling to acting, as well as finding love. This is the last drama that Park Bo-gum acted in before joining the military!

Original air dates in South Korea: September 7–October 27, 2020 (16 episodes) **Cast:** Park Bo-gum (Sa Hye Jun), So-dam Park (Ahn Jeong Ha)

Chocolate

Cool neurosurgeon Lee Kang and soft hearted chef Cha Yeong heal each other's souls via cooking in this romantic drama.

Original air dates in South Korea: November 29, 2019–January 9, 2020 (16 episodes) **Cast:** Ha Ji-Won (Moon Cha Yeong), Yoon Kyesang (Lee Kang)

When the Camellia Blooms

A thriller–love story about Oh Dong Baek, a single mother who opens a bar in a small town, and Yong Sik, the police officer who falls in love with her.

Original air dates in South Korea: September 18–November 21, 2019 (40 episodes) **Cast:** Kong Hyo-Jin (Oh Dong Baek), Kang Ha-neul (Hwang Yong Sik)

Hi Bye, Mama!

Yu Ri, who died in a tragic accident, is given the chance to become human again through a reincarnation project. However, her husband is remarried and has built a new family!

Original air dates in South Korea: February 22–April 19, 2020 (16 episodes) **Cast:** Kim Tae hee (Cha Yu Ri), Kyoo-hyung Lee (Cho Gang Hwa)

Something in the Rain

A single woman in her thirties reunites with the younger brother of her best friend, who has just returned from overseas and dormant feelings of love are reawakened. The realistic depiction of their relationship caused quite a stir!

Original air dates in South Korea: March 30–May 19, 2018 (16 episodes) **Cast:** Jung Hae-In (Seo Joon Hee), Son Ye-jin (Yoon Jin-Ah)

Romance is a Bonus Book

Thirty-seven-year-old Dan Yi has lost her house, her money and her husband. In order to have a roof over her head, she goes to editor Eun Ho, who is like a younger brother to her, and starts living with him.

Original air dates in South Korea: January 26–March 17, 2019 (16 episodes) **Cast:** Lee Na-Young (Kang Dan Yi), Lee Jong-Suk (Cha Eun Ho)

Was It Love?

A romance that depicts the complicated relationships between a single mother who has been a stranger to love for a long time, and four handsome men with a comedic touch.

Original air dates in South Korea: July 8–September 2, 2020 (16 episodes) **Cast:** Song Ji-Hyo (Noh Ae Jeong), Ho Joon Son (Oh Dae Oh)

Chapter 1

Classic Korean Dishes that Appear in K-dramas

Soft Tofu Stew Sundubu Jjigae 순두부찌개

Serves 1
PREPARATION TIME: 20 minutes

- 1 teaspoon light soy sauce
- 1 teaspoon salt
- 1 small piece silken tofu
- 1¼ cups (300 ml) water
- 3 tablespoons Dadaegi Spicy Meat
  Sauce (see page 115 for recipe;
  and note below)
- 4 medium shrimp
- 4 fresh scallops
- Minced green onions, to taste
- 1 medium egg
- 1 teaspoon salted shrimp, or 1
  teaspoon dashi stock granules

1 Sprinkle the soy sauce and salt on the silken tofu to draw out the moisture. Since tofu exudes moisture when it's put into soup, it's important to draw out the moisture beforehand.

2 Put the water and Dadaegi Spicy Meat Sauce in a pan and heat.

3 When the pan comes to a boil, add the tofu from Step 1, the shrimp and the scallops.

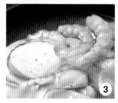

4 When the pan comes back to a boil, add the minced green onions and break in the egg. Season with the salted shrimp or dashi stock granules, bring back to a boil again and serve.

Note Dadaegi is a spicy sauce (see page 115) that is used frequently in Korean soups and hot pots. If you make it in quantity, it's really convenient to have on hand when you want to add some flavor to whatever you're making.

The Soft Tofu Stew at Danbam, the Bar-Restaurant in *Itaewon Class*

This is the star dish at the Danbam bar-restaurant. It appears in the scene where the head chef Ma Hyun Yi wins the TV show *The Best Food Stall*, and there's also a scene where Sae Ro Yi serves this dish to the chairman of the Jangga Group.

Potato Pancakes Gamjajeon 감자전

Makes 5–6 4-inch (10 cm) diameter pancakes
PREPARATION TIME: 20 minutes

2 medium potatoes
Salt, to taste
2 tablespoons vegetable oil
1 tablespoon sesame oil

FOR THE DIPPING SAUCE
All-purpose Korean-style Soy Sauce (page 108), to taste
Minced green onions, to taste

1 Peel the potatoes, and finely shred one of them. Grate the other potato, and squeeze the moisture out lightly with your hands.

2 Put the shredded and grated potatoes into a bowl, add salt, and mix well while squeezing with your hands.

3 Heat the oil in a frying pan or on a griddle over medium heat, then place rounds of the Step 2 mixture onto the hot surface.

4 When the pancakes are browned on one side, flip them over and cook the other side.

5 Serve with the All-purpose Korean-style Soy Sauce-based Sauce mixed with the minced green onions.

Note In South Korea, potato pancakes are eaten as a snack rather than with a meal. In order to cook them to a crispy finish, use a generous amount of oil and don't worry about the calories! These are delicious topped with melted cheese too.

The Potato Pancakes In Episode 3 of *Crash Landing on You*

A group of housewives come to inspect the woman who from the "south" who calls herself Jeong-hyeok's fiancée. They bring potato pancakes as a gift, as an excuse to get into the house.

Photofest/アフロ

Japchae Noodles

Japchae 잡채

Serves 2 to 3
PREPARATION TIME: 50 minutes

4 oz (110 g) dried dangmyeon
  noodles or dried glass or
  cellophane noodles
½ bell pepper
½ onion
¼ carrot
Small handful dried wood ear
  mushrooms, about 2 g
2 oz (60 g) thinly sliced beef
Vegetable oil, for stir-frying
Sesame seeds, to taste

SEASONING MIX A
½ teaspoon soy sauce
½ teaspoon light corn syrup
  (or 1 teaspoon sugar)
1 teaspoon grated garlic
½ teaspoon sesame oil

SEASONING MIX B
1½ tablespoons soy sauce
1 tablespoon ume plum essence,
  or ½ tablespoon sugar
1 tablespoon vegetable oil
½ teaspoon grated garlic

1 Cook the noodles following the directions on the packet. Drain. Shred the bell pepper, onion and carrot. Rehydrate the wood ear mushrooms by soaking them in water until softened.

2 Combine the beef with Seasoning Mix A, and leave to marinate for about 30 minutes.

3 Put the vegetable oil in a frying pan and stir-fry the vegetables. Stir-fry the beef in another frying pan, then transfer both to one bowl when cooked.

4 Combine the Seasoning Mix B ingredients in a pan and bring to a boil. Add the noodles and simmer for about 10 minutes. Mix the noodles with the vegetables and beef, and sprinkle with sesame seeds to serve.

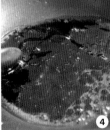

Note The type of noodles typically used for japchae are dangmyeon, which are made with sweet potato starch and are rather thick. It's worthwhile seeking these out for the best results. Prevent the noodles from turning limp by simmering them in All-Purpose Korean-style Soy Sauce (page 108) beforehand. You can use whatever vegetables you have in your refrigerator! If you stir-fry the vegetables separately from the noodles, they won't become too wilted.

The Japchae in Episode 1 of *Record of Youth*

Hye Jun doesn't want to give up on his dream of becoming an actor, and works at temporary jobs every day. On the other hand, in Hye Jun's family, money is important. In this episode, japchae appears in an elaborate family meal over which his father's money-making schemes are discussed.

Everett Collection/アフロ

Korean Barbecue Samgyeopsal 삼겹살

Serves 2
PREPARATION TIME: 20 minutes

12 oz (350 g) thickly cut pork belly slices
Garlic, to taste, sliced thinly
Kimchi, to taste
Cheese, to taste

FOR THE MISO SAUCE
1 tablespoon doenjang soybean paste, or red miso paste
1 tablespoon unsweetened peanut butter
1 tablespoon light corn syrup or honey
1 tablespoon ume plum essence (or ½ tablespoon sugar)

FOR THE DIPPING SAUCE
Sesame oil
Salt and pepper

TO SERVE
Loose leaf lettuce
Perilla leaves

1 Cut the pork belly slices into bite-sized pieces.

2 Spread out the pork pieces in a heated frying pan or griddle and cook on both sides until browned.

3 Add the sliced garlic, kimchi and cheese to the pan or griddle as the pork is cooking and cook them too.

4 Wipe up the excess fat that comes out of the pork with a wadded up paper towel (in Korea a piece of sliced bread is used for this purpose too).

5 Mix the miso sauce ingredients together.

6 Mix the dipping sauce ingredients together.

7 Each diner spreads out a piece of lettuce and a perilla leaf or two, and tops it with the cooked pork, garlic, miso sauce, and toppings of their choice. The whole thing is wrapped and dipped into the dipping sauce to eat.

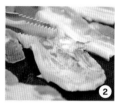

Note Mature kimchi that has been fermented for a while is recommended for this dish. The sour flavor will counteract the oiliness of the pork. The Korean way to eat this is to eat the leafy wrap in one bite with gusto! All the ingredients combine in your mouth for a flavor explosion!

The Korean Barbecue in Episode 5 of *Hospital Playlist*

This drama is about five doctors who went to medical school together and now work at the same hospital. They relax from the stresses of their day in the band they have formed. One day after work, they go for Korean barbecue before starting band rehearsals.

Everett Collection/アフロ

Steamed Eggs Gyeran-jjim 계란찜

Serves 2
PREPARATION TIME: 20 minutes

2 teaspoons sesame oil, divided
3 eggs
2 oz (60 g) salted pollack roe
2 tablespoons sliced green onion or leek
1 teaspoon salted shrimp, or light soy sauce
⅔ cup (150 ml) dasima or kombu dashi stock (make by soaking a 2 inch long piece of dasima or kombu seaweed in water for at least an hour)
Sesame seeds, for sprinkling

1 Coat the inside of a pot (an earthenware pot is preferred) evenly with 1 teaspoon of sesame oil.

2 Break the eggs into a bowl. Skin the salted pollack roe, and set aside a third of it to use as a topping, along with a third of the sliced green onions. Add the rest of the pollack roe and green onions as well as the salted shrimp or soy sauce to the eggs and mix well.

3 Put the dashi stock in the pot over high heat. When it comes to the boil, swirl in the Step 2 mixture slowly. Turn the heat down to low and mix with chopsticks so that the soup mixture does not burn.

4 When the eggs have cooked through slightly, turn off the heat. Top with the reserved pollack roe and green onions, cover with a lid and leave for 5 minutes.

5 Sprinkle with the sesame seeds and the re-maining 1 teaspoon of sesame oil.

Note If you spread the inside of the pot with sesame oil before adding the dashi stock to it, the eggs are less likely to burn and will take on a nutty flavor. You can use readymade dashi stock instead of soaking the kombu seaweed in water. Be sure to eat this as soon as it's made, or the eggs will shrivel up!

The Steamed Eggs in Episode 10 of *When the Camellia Blooms*

Yong Sik helps his mother out at her home. His mother serves him piping hot steamed eggs. Even though they complain at each other all the time, you can feel the love between mother and son in this scene.

Bibimbap Bibimbap 비빔밥

Serves 2
PREPARATION TIME: 1 hour

1 cup (100 g) mung bean sprouts

SEASONING MIX A

1 teaspoon sesame oil
1 teaspoon minced green onions
½ teaspoon salt

1 small Japanese cucumber
Salt, for sprinkling

SEASONING MIX B

1 teaspoon sesame oil
½ teaspoon salt
1 teaspoon toasted sesame
    seeds

½ carrot
1 teaspoon vegetable oil
1 teaspoon grated garlic
½ teaspoon salt
4 oz (110 g) king oyster
    mushrooms
1 teaspoon vegetable oil

SEASONING MIX C

1 teaspoon soy sauce
½ teaspoon sugar
1 teaspoon sesame oil

SEASONING MIX D

1 tablespoon soy sauce
½ tablespoon sugar
2 teaspoons grated garlic
1 teaspoon sesame oil
Black pepper, to taste

5 oz (150 g) ground beef
1 teaspoon vegetable oil
2 eggs

**GOCHUJANG WITH PEANUT
    BUTTER**

1 tablespoon unsweetened
    peanut butter
2 tablespoons gochujang
1 tablespoon honey
1 teaspoon sesame oil
1 teaspoon chopped peanuts

1½ cups (300 g) hot cooked rice
Sesame oil, to taste

1 Blanch the bean sprouts in boiling water and drain well. Put the Seasoning Mix A ingredients in a bowl and mix with the cooked bean sprouts.

2 Slice the cucumber thinly and sprinkle with salt. Leave until wilted, then squeeze out the excess moisture. Put the Put the Seasoning Mix B ingredients in a bowl and mix with the cucumber.

3 Shred the carrot and stir-fry in the vegetable oil over medium heat with the garlic. Season with the salt.

4 Blanch the king oyster mushrooms in boiling water and drain well. Stir-fry in 1 teaspoon of vegetable oil

over medium heat, then transfer to a bowl and combine with the Seasoning Mix C ingredients.

5 Rub the Seasoning Mix D ingredients into the ground beef. Put the 1 teaspoon of vegetable oil in a frying pan and stir-fry the beef over medium heat until there is no moisture left in the pan.

6 Fry the eggs. Mix the Gochujang with Peanut Butter ingredients. Divide the rice between two bowls, and top with the toppings made in steps 1–5 and the fried eggs. Garnish with sesame oil and the Gochujang with Peanut Butter.

The Bibimbap in Episode 3 of *Romance is a Bonus Book*

Eun Ho and Dan Yi grew up together like brother and sister. Dan Yi, who has lost her husband and her house, secretly breaks into Eun Ho's house. Several days later Dan Yi is discovered by Eun Ho, and sulks while eating a bowl of bibimbap.

Everett Collection/アフロ

Boiled Pork Wraps Bossam 보쌈

Serves 2
PREPARATION TIME: 1 hour

**1 block of pork belly, about
    1 lb (450 g)
Water for soaking
6 cups (1.5 L) water**

INGREDIENTS A

**½ onion
Green parts of 1 leek or large
    green onion
5 garlic cloves
Small piece of ginger, peeled
1 tablespoon doenjang soybean
    paste, or red miso paste
2 tablespoons soy sauce
1 tablespoon instant coffee
    granules**

TO SERVE

**10 loose leaf lettuce leaves
1 tablespoon salted shrimp
Kimchi, to taste
Sliced garlic, to taste
1 teaspoon sesame oil**

1 Soak the pork belly block in water to cover for 30 minutes to an hour to get rid of the blood.

2 Put the 6 cups of water in a deep pot. Add the soaked pork belly and the A ingredients, cover with a lid and heat over high heat. When the pot comes to a boil simmer the pork belly for 30 to 40 minutes over medium heat. When a skewer or toothpick goes through the meat easily it is done.

3 Cut the pork into ½ inch (1 cm) wide slices, and arrange on a plate with the lettuce leaves, salted shrimp, kimchi and sliced garlic. Sprinkle with the sesame oil. Eat by wrapping the meat and your favorite seasoning in a lettuce leaf.

Note Since the excess fat falls away when the pork is boiled, this is a very healthy dish. But you can still taste the great flavor of the pork, which is enhanced by the salted shrimp, kimchi and garlic.

The Boiled Pork Wraps in Episode 7 of *Mystic Pop-up Bar*

Kang Bae has won the dance contest. He asks the chairman to have a drink with him, and the chairman agrees. The dish he serves to the chairman on that occasion is boiled pork wraps. When the chairman falls asleep, Kang Bae visits the chairman's dreams and realizes there is a big misunderstanding.

Everett Collection/アフロ

Beef Bone Soup  Gomtang 곰탕

Serves 4
PREPARATION TIME: 1 hour

¼ daikon radish, about 4 oz
   (110 g)
1 large green onion or leek
Beef shank, about 1 lb 12 oz
2 pieces of kombu seaweed,
   each 2 inches (5 cm) square
6 cups (1.5 L) water
Leek or green onion, for garnish
Salt and pepper, to taste

1 Cut the daikon radish and large green onion or leek into smaller pieces so that they fit into a pot. Put the beef, kombu seaweed and water into the pot and turn the heat to high.

2 When the pot comes to a boil, take out the kombu seaweed and lower the heat to medium. Skim off any scum.

3 After about 1 hour, take out the daikon radish and green onion or leek. Take out the beef and slice into easy-to-eat pieces. Reserve the soup.

4 Arrange the beef in a bowl and pour the soup over it. Garnish with some chopped green onion or leek, and add salt and pepper to taste.

Note Although this resembles seolleongtang, another beef soup, gomtang is lighter. It is often eaten the morning after drinking too much, as a hangover cure! It's also eaten with rice in a dish called gomtang gukbap.

The Beef Bone Soup in Episode 6 of *Familiar Wife*

This dish makes an appearance when Jong Hoo goes out for lunch with Woo-jin. Joo-hyuk comes and spends lunch time with them. When Jong-hoo cuts up the kimchi or tries to fetch water for Woo-jin, Joo-hyuk gets in the way.

Ginseng Chicken Soup Samgyetang 삼계탕

Serves 1
PREPARATION TIME: 50 minutes

3 to 4 tablespoons uncooked short grain or mochi rice
Water for soaking
1 ginseng root
2 dried red dates
1 small chicken
3 garlic cloves
6 cups (1.5 L) water
1 large green onion or leek
5 whole black peppercorns
Salt and pepper, to taste

1 Put the rice in a bowl, and soak it in water for about 1 hour. Wash the ginseng and the dried red dates. Cut the neck, wings and the tail fat off the chicken, and rinse the inside well. Pat dry with paper towels.

2 Stuff the cavity of the chicken with the soaked rice (to about 80% since the rice will swell when cooking), as well as the garlic and red dates to stop the rice from coming out.

3 Close up the cavity on the top and bottom so the stuffings do not leak out. Either make a small hole with scissors on the base of one leg, and insert the other leg into the hole; alternatively, cross the legs and tie them together with kitchen twine.

4 Put the 6 cups of water in a pot. Add the stuffed chicken, the ginseng, the green parts of the green onion (which eliminate gaminess from the chicken) and the peppercorns. (Reserve the remaining green onion for the garnish.) Turn the heat to high. When the pot comes to a boil turn the heat down to medium, and simmer with a lid on for about 50 minutes while skimming off any scum.

5 Remove the chicken from the soup and place in a serving bowl. Strain the soup through a colander and pour it over the chicken. Season the soup with salt and pepper and serve garnished with chopped leek or green onion.

Note This soup warms up the body in winter, and is eaten in the summer for energy when the weather is hot. It is also delicious garnished with ginger, pine nuts, goji berries and shredded dried chili pepper.

The Ginseng Chicken Soup in Episode 10 of *Familiar Wife*

📺 The KCU Bank holds a marathon. Woo-jin mistakenly thinks that Jong Hoo has collapsed, and realizes her feelings for him for the first time. The team finishes well in third place, and they all go out for ginseng chicken soup to celebrate. However, Woo-jin, normally a strong drinker, ends up getting drunk.

Seaweed Soup with Beef Miyeokguk 미역국

Serves 2
PREPARATION TIME: 20 minutes

¼ cup (20 g) dried seaweed
  (miyeok or wakame)
Water for soaking
4 oz (110 g) thinly sliced beef
  shank
2 tablespoons salted anchovy
  extract, or light soy sauce,
  divided
1 tablespoon sesame oil
3½ cups (800 ml) water
1 teaspoon salt

1 Soak the dried seaweed in water to rehydrate it, then rinse it and drain. Cut the beef into bite-sized pieces.

2 Put the beef into a pan, sprinkle with 1 tablespoon of the salted anchovy extract and cook while stirring for about 3 minutes over medium heat. Add the seaweed and sesame oil and stir-fry some more. Add the 3½ cups water and turn the heat to high.

3 When the pan comes to a boil, add the salt and the remaining 1 tablespoon of salted anchovy extract (or slightly less, to taste) and simmer for about 10 more minutes before serving, while skimming off any scum.

Note This seaweed soup is traditionally served on birthdays in Korea. If you can get hold of salted anchovy extract to season it, the flavor will be really authentic.

The Seaweed Soup with Beef in Episode 10 of
Hi Bye, Mama!

Yu Ri dies suddenly. Her family can't accept it, and they make a big pot of seaweed soup with beef for her. Her mother Eun Suk won't let anyone touch it. Yu Ri's husband Gang Hwa throws the soup away, then apologizes to Eun Suk.

Everett Collection/アフロ

Korean Ingredients to Up Your Korean Cooking Game!

Seasonings that add depth of flavor

The three ingredients featured on this page are the Korean seasonings that it's hard to find the perfect substitute for, so do your best to get a hold of them for a really authentic flavor! You should be able to find them easily at your local Korean grocery store or Asian market.

Salted shrimp

Called saeu-jeot in Korean, these tiny shrimps have been salted and fermented. They are a great way of adding richness and umami to dishes and are an indispensable ingredient in the base sauce for kimchi (see page 88). You'll also find salted shrimp in other recipes, such as for Soft Tofu Stew (page 13), Steamed Eggs (page 20) and Spicy Braised Tofu (page 124). There really is no substitute for this ingredient.

Salted anchovy extract

Called myeolchijeot in Korean, salted anchovy extract is a type of fish sauce, made by salting anchovies, fermenting them and extracting just the essence. It is used to make kimchi, as well as in stir-fries, fried dishes, hot pots and soup. You'll find salted anchovy extract called for in the recipes for Seaweed Soup with Beef (page 31), Noodle Soup (page 35), Kimchi Sauce (page 88) and others. If you can't find it, use light soy sauce instead.

Green plum extract

Called maesil-cheong in Korean, this uniquely Korean seasoning is used to add a sweet plum flavor to dishes while eliminating any gaminess. Green plum extract is used in the recipes for Spicy Stir-fried Pork (page 39), Braised Mackerel with Daikon (page 49), Dried Squid with Chili (page 121) and others. Sugar can be used as a substitute—see each recipe for the equivalent amount.

Chapter 2

Dishes that Have a Starring Role in K-dramas

The Noodle Soup Recipe in Episode 16 of *Crash Landing on You*

Before he returns to North Korea Jeong-hyeok is worried about Se-ri's irregular schedule. He writes down the recipes for crispy rice and for noodle soup and sticks them on the refrigerator door. Seeing them makes Se-ri happy, although she still feels lonely.

Noodle Soup Guksu 국수

Serves 2
PREPARATION TIME: 30 minutes

**FOR THE DRIED-ANCHOVY STOCK
(MAKES MORE THAN NEEDED)**
1 oz (30 g) dried anchovies
  (myeolchi or niboshi)
8¼ cups (2 L) water
Piece of dried dasima or kombu
  seaweed, about 4 inches (10
  cm) square

FOR THE NOODLE SOUP
¼ large green onion or leek
1 red chili pepper
¼ onion
¼ zucchini
¼ carrot

1 dried shiitake mushroom,
  reconstituted
2½ cups (600 ml) dried-anchovy
  stock (see above), prepared a
  day in advance
1 tablespoon doenjang soybean
  paste, or red miso paste
1 tablespoon salted anchovy
  extract, or light soy sauce
7 oz (200 g) somyeon or somen
  noodles

FOR THE EGG CREPE
1 egg
Pinch of salt
Oil for frying

1 Make the dried-anchovy stock a day in advance. Dry-roast the anchovies in an unoiled frying pan over medium heat until they have a nutty fragrance.

2 Put the water in a pan and bring to a boil. Add the anchovies and kombu and turn off the heat. Leave the pan overnight, then sieve.

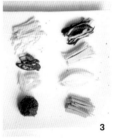

3

3 Cut the green onion or leek and red chili pepper into thin diagonal slices. Slice the onion thinly, and shred the zucchini, carrot, and reconstituted dried shiitake mushroom.

4 Put the anchovy stock in a pan and bring to a boil. Dissolve the doenjang in it.

4

5 Add the vegetables from Step 3 to the broth. When it comes back to a boil add the salted anchovy extract or light soy sauce to season.

6 Cook the noodles in a separate pan, rinse in plenty of cold water, and drain well.

7 To make the crepe, beat the egg and salt together. Cook into thin crepes in 2 to 3 batches in an oiled frying pan.

8 Put the somyeon or somen noodles in a bowl and pour over the Step 5 broth. Garnish with thinly sliced egg crepe.

Note In South Korea, noodles are often served at celebratory occasions as a sign of longevity. When cooked somyeon or somen noodles are rinsed they turn cold, so it's best if you warm them up again. In the summer they are also delicious served in a cold broth.

Crispy Rice Nurungji 누룽지

Serves 2
PREPARATION TIME: 30 minutes

1 cup (200 g) cold cooked rice
3 tablespoons water
Sugar, to taste

1 Put the rice in a frying pan, and spread it out to about ¼ inch (5 mm) in thickness while adding the water.

2 Press down on the rice to crush the grains, and cook for about 20 minutes until the underside of the rice is browned.

3 When the rice is crispy and can be peeled off the frying pan it is done. Arrange on a plate and eat sprinkled with some sugar.

Note Using cold cooked rice for this dish gives a crispier result than freshly cooked hot rice. In the drama they ate the crispy rice as a sweet snack with sugar. You can also add tea to it to soften it into a dish known as sungnyung—scorched rice tea—which is sometimes served at the end of a meal in Korea.

The Crispy Rice Recipe in Episode 16 of *Crash Landing on You*

Rich girl Se-ri used to be called the "Small Appetite Princess" since she would only eat three mouthfuls of food even at a Michelin-starred restaurant, but she really got into crispy rice in North Korea. Before he leaves Seoul, Jeong-hyeok leaves Se-ri the recipe so that she can make it herself.

Photofest/게티

Spicy Stir-fried Pork Dwaejigogi Bokkeum 제육볶음

Serves 2
PREPARATION TIME: 30 minutes

**12 oz (350 g) thinly sliced pork
 belly
1 tablespoon sake or cheongju
1 tablespoon grated ginger
1 onion
2 large green onions
¼ carrot
1 teaspoon grated garlic
1 teaspoon sesame oil**

**SEASONING MIX
1 tablespoon gochujang paste
1 tablespoon chili powder
2 tablespoons soy sauce
2 tablespoons green plum
 extract, or 1 tablespoon sugar
1 tablespoon light corn syrup or
 honey
1 tablespoon water**

1 Cut the pork belly into bite-sized pieces. Put into a bowl with the sake and grated ginger, and rub the seasonings well into the pork with your hands.

2 Cut the onion into wedges, and slice the green onions and carrot thinly.

3 Put the Seasoning Mix ingredients into another bowl and mix well.

4 Heat a frying pan, put in the Step 1 pork, as well as the carrot and grated garlic, and stir-fry.

5 When the meat changes color add the Step 3 ingredients and stir-fry until the meat is cooked.

6 Add the onion and green onion, and stir-fry quickly. Drizzle in the sesame oil and turn off the heat.

Note Gochujang and syrup burn easily, so be careful. It's best to add them after the other ingredients are mostly cooked. This is an easy yet satisfying dish, which is great served with rice.

The Spicy Stir-fried Pork in Episode 4 of *When the Camellia Blooms*

This is the signature dish at Camellia, the small bar-restaurant operated by Dong Baek. Her first love, Jong Ryul, loves it and devours it with rice.

Everett Collection/アフロ

Korean Tonkatsu

Donkkaseu 한국식 돈까스

Serves 1
PREPARATION TIME: 30 minutes

1 piece pork shoulder cutlet,
  about 4 oz (110 g)
Salt and pepper, to taste
1 tablespoon grated garlic
Salt and pepper
¾ cup (100 g) tempura flour or
  plain flour
1 egg
1 cup (60 g) panko breadcrumbs
Vegetable oil for deep-frying

SAUCE (MAKES EXTRA)
2 tablespoons butter
2 tablespoons flour
3 tablespoons Worcestershire
  sauce
3 tablespoons ketchup
½ cup (120 ml) water
¼ cup (70 ml) milk
½ tablespoon of sugar

1 Wrap the pork cutlet in cling film, and bash it with a rolling pin to make it about ⅛ inch (3 mm) thick. Salt and pepper both sides of the pork, and spread evenly with the grated garlic.

2 Put the flour, beaten egg and panko bread-crumbs in separate flat containers or dishes.

3 Spread out the pork piece and dip it into the flour, then into the beaten egg, then into the panko breadcrumbs.

4 Heat the oil to 360°F (180°C), and put the pork in slowly. Fry until golden brown on both sides, and drain off the excess oil.

5 While the pork is cooking, make the sauce. Heat a frying pan over low heat, add the butter then the flour, and sauté until the flour is browned. Mix in the Worcestershire sauce and ketchup, then the water and milk, and cook until thickened. Any leftover sauce will keep refrigerated for a couple of days, or up to a month in the freezer.

6 Arrange the pork cutlet on a plate, and pour over the sauce.

Note This is a Korean version of the Japanese fried pork cutlet, tonkatsu. In South Korea a large, thin cutlet is usually served with a thick demiglace sauce. A soju bottle is often used to flatten out the meat!

The Tonkatsu in Episode 5 of *Familiar Wife*

Joo-hyuk and Woo-jin visit a tonkatsu restaurant they used to go to when they first met. Joo-hyuk says "the tonkatsu here is as amazing as the ending of *The Lion King*" while he digs into the said dish, and thinks back nostalgically to when Woo-jin was younger.

Octopus Stir-fry with Spices Nakji-bokkeum 낙지볶음

Serves 2
PREPARATION TIME: 30 minutes

1 lb (450 g) raw octopus or squid
Flour, for sprinkling
½ onion
2 large green onions
2 tablespoons vegetable oil
1 teaspoon sesame oil

SEASONING MIX
3 tablespoons soy sauce
1 tablespoon chili pepper
   powder
1 tablespoon gochujang paste
2 tablespoons green plum
   extract, or 1 tablespoon sugar
1 tablespoon light corn syrup
1 tablespoon grated garlic

1 Start by turning the octopus head inside out and taking out the innards. Sprinkle the octopus evenly with flour, and rub the suckers vigorously to remove any sliminess. Put the octopus in a pot of boiling water and boil for a few minutes. Cut into 3½ inch (8 cm) pieces.

2 Cut the onion in half and slice into 6 wedges. Cut the green onions into 4 inch (10 cm) pieces and shred.

3 Heat the vegetable oil in a frying pan, add the green onion and stir-fry briefly to make green onion oil. Add the onion wedges and the Seasoning Mix ingredients, and stir-fry over medium heat.

4 Add the octopus and stir-fry. (Be careful not to over-cook the octopus or it will become tough!)

5 Turn off the heat and drizzle in the sesame oil. Mix rapidly and arrange the contents of the pan on a plate.

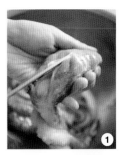

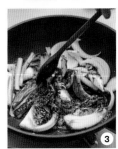

Note Boiling the octopus before stir-frying prevents it from becoming watery, and helps it retain flavor. If you can't get hold of octopus, this is delicious made with squid too!

The Octopus Stir-fry with Spices in Episode 3 of
Mystic Pop-up Bar

A young man comes to the Mystic Pop-up Bar and eats octopus stir-fry with spices while crying. He graduated at the top of his class from university and is looking for work. Although he got a perfect score in the written section of the employment test for a job at a hotel, he was still turned down. Is it because of some shenanigans going in the background?

Everett Collection/アフロ

Dishes that Have a Starring Role in K-dramas   43

Korean Corn Dogs Hasdogeu 핫도그

Makes 10 corn dogs
PREPARATION TIME: 30 minutes

5 hot dog sausages (or similar
  sausages), cut in half
5 cups (300 g) fresh
  breadcrumbs
Vegetable oil for deep-frying

FOR THE BATTER
1¼ cups (150 g) pancake mix
2¾ tablespoons milk
1 egg

SEASONINGS
Sugar, to taste
Ketchup, to taste
Mustard, to taste

* You'll also need 10 bamboo
  skewers

1 Skewer the sausage halves on the bamboo skewers.

2 Make the batter. Put all the batter ingredients in a bowl, and whisk together until there are no lumps.

3 Coat the sausages liberally with the batter, then coat in the fresh breadcrumbs.

4 Heat the oil to 340°F (170°C) and deep-fry the sausages.

5 When the sausages are golden brown, take them out of the oil. Serve with sugar, ketchup or mustard to taste.

Note I recommend using fresh breadcrumbs, which will become thick and crunchy. The batter should be on the stiff side to coat the sausages well, so if it's too loose add a little extra pancake mix.

The Corn Dogs in Episode 2 of *Start-Up*

Ji Pyung and Dal Mi's grandmother, Won Deok, meet again for the first time in a while. Ji Pyung eats the corn dogs Won Deok serves from her food cart, and proposes to pay her back for the past, but he is turned down.

Everett Collection/

Stir-fried Pork and Bean Sprouts

Samgyupsal Sukju Bokkeum 돼지고기숙주볶음

Serves 2
PREPARATION TIME: 20 minutes

½ large green onion
½ tablespoon vegetable oil
½ tablespoon grated garlic
½ pound (250 g) thinly sliced pork belly
1½ cups (150 g) bean sprouts

SEASONING MIX
2 tablespoons soy sauce
½ tablespoon oyster sauce
½ tablespoon green plum extract, or ½ tablespoon sugar
½ tablespoon sesame oil

1 Slice the green onion thinly.

2 Put the Seasoning Mix ingredients in a bowl and mix to combine.

3 Heat a frying pan and put in the oil. Stir-fry the green onion and grated garlic over medium heat.

4 When the green onion is fragrant add the pork, turn the heat to high, and stir-fry.

5 When the pork is cooked and has changed color, add the bean sprouts and the Step 2 ingredients, and stir-fry quickly over high heat.

Note Although this goes well with rice as part of a meal, in South Korea it's a popular drinking appetizer. The key is to stir-fry the bean sprouts quickly over high heat, so that they don't wilt. This is delicious with some chili pepper added too.

The Stir-fried Pork and Bean Sprouts in Episode 7 of *Itaewon Class*

The chairman of the Jangga Group visits the Danbam bar-restaurant with Soo Ah and Geun Won and asks for a stir-fried dish that the restaurant recommends. Sae Ro Yi orders the staff to make stir-fried pork and bean sprouts.

Braised Mackerel with Daikon Godeungeo Jorim 고등어조림

Serves 2
PREPARATION TIME: 40 minutes

1 daikon radish, about 1 lb
   (450 g)
1 onion
1 piece ginger
2 mackerel
1 large green onion

SEASONING MIX
3 tablespoons chili powder
1 tablespoon soy sauce
1 tablespoon salted anchovy
   extract, or Thai fish sauce
1 tablespoon mirin, or
   ½ tablespoon sugar
1 tablespoon green plum extract,
   or ½ tablespoon sugar
1 tablespoon grated garlic
3 tablespoons sake or cheongju
Black pepper, to taste
¾ cup (200 ml) water

1 Peel the daikon radish, cut into half lengthwise, and slice into ½ inch (1 cm) wide pieces. Slice the onion thinly. Peel the ginger and shred finely.

2 Take the intestines out of the mackerel and rinse with water until clean. Make several cuts in the skin so that the flavors will penetrate it.

3 Put all the Seasoning Mix ingredients in a bowl and mix well.

4 Line the bottom of a pan with the sliced daikon radish, and put the mackerel on top of it. Add the onion and ginger. Add the Seasoning Mix ingredients from Step 3, cover with a lid and cook over high heat.

5 After cooking for about 10 minutes, take the lid off and lower the heat to medium. Simmer for another 10 minutes while spooning the liquid over the mackerel.

6 Cut up the green onion diagonally, and add to the pan. Cover with a lid again and simmer for about 5 minutes over low heat.

Note Simmered mackerel is a staple of Korean cooking. By lining the bottom of the pan with daikon radish the mackerel are less likely to burn, and the mix of flavors is delicious too. This recipe also works well with other fish such as Spanish mackerel or beltfish.

The Braised Mackerel with Daikon in Episode 3 of *Chocolate*

While Cha Yeong is eating dinner at a restaurant close to the hospice, an order for braised mackerel with daikon comes in on the phone. The owner is dismayed because he has forgotten how to make it, but Cha Yeong shows off her skills by cooking the dish.

Cold Noodles with Beef Naengmyeon 냉면

Serves 2
PREPARATION TIME: 1 hour

3½ cups (800 ml) cold Beef Bone
    Soup (see page 27)
4 thin slices of boiled beef shank,
    about 3 oz (80 g) total
½ Asian pear
1 small or ½ large cucumber
1 teaspoon salt
1 hard-boiled egg
2 servings naengmyeon noodles,
    about 6 oz (170 g) per serving
Mustard, to taste
Vinegar, to taste

SEASONING
2 tablespoons vinegar
2 tablespoons sugar
2 teaspoons light soy sauce
2 teaspoons salt

1 Put all the Seasoning ingredients into the beef bone soup. Mix well and chill.

2 Slice the boiled beef shank and the pear thinly. Slice the cucumber diagonally, rub in the salt, leave for 10 minutes then squeeze out tightly. Cut the hard-boiled egg in half.

3 Cook the naengmyeon noodles following the directions on the packet. When cooked, rinse well under running water until they are no longer sticky, and drain well.

4 Put the noodles into bowls, top with the cucumber, pear, beef shank and hard-boiled egg. Pour the soup over, taking care not to let the mounds of vegetables and meat and egg fall apart. Add mustard and vinegar if you want.

Note Naengmyeon noodles contain buckwheat flour, and are available at Korean grocery stores. This soup is also delicious made with somyeon or somen noodles. This beef soup made from beef shank is very Korean. Use whatever toppings you like!

The Cold Noodles in Episode 12 of *One Spring Night*

When Jung-in is about to go out with friends for cold noodles, she runs into Ji Ho's mother Sook-hee and his son Eun Woo by chance. When Ji Ho later asks his mother what she thought about Jung-in, she says, "She's beautiful and seems level-headed," which makes him smile.

Noodles in Spicy Black Bean Sauce

Jajangmyeon 짜장면

Serves 2
PREPARATION TIME: 30 minutes

¼ onion
¼ zucchini
½ small or ¼ large cucumber
4 oz (110 g) thinly sliced pork
    shoulder
1 teaspoon grated ginger
1 teaspoon salt
Pepper, to taste
1 tablespoon chili oil
1 tablespoon grated garlic
Cornstarch water (½ teaspoon
    cornstarch mixed with 1
    tablespoon water)
2 servings dried Chinese egg
    noodles, about 4 oz (120 g) per
    serving
Red chili pepper powder, to taste

FOR THE BLACK BEAN SAUCE
¾ cup (200 ml) water
5 tablespoons chunjang (Korean
    black bean paste) or tianmian
    (Chinese fermented sweet
    bean sauce)
1 tablespoon sugar
1 tablespoon red chili pepper
    powder

1 Chop the onion and zucchini roughly. Shred the cucumber.

2 Cut the pork into bite-sized pieces. Mix with the grated ginger, salt and pepper.

3 Make the black bean sauce. Combine all the sauce ingredients in a bowl and mix well.

4 Put the chili oil in a frying pan and add the pork from Step 2 and the grated garlic and stir-fry over high heat. When the meat changes color add the onion and zucchini from Step 1 and stir-fry until the vegetables are cooked.

5 Add the sauce from Step 3 and stir-fry for about 3 minutes. Drizzle in the cornstarch water a little at a time to thicken the sauce.

6 Cook the noodles, rinse under running water and drain well.

7 Arrange the noodles on plates, pour over the Step 5 sauce, and top with the shredded cucumber. Sprinkle on some red chili pepper to taste.

Note This is a Korean version of a Chinese dish. You could call it soul food for Korean people. It's also delicious made with rice instead of noodles and topped with a fried egg.

The Noodles in Spicy Black Bean Sauce in Episode 7 of *Hospital Playlist*

Joon Wan and Ik Soon, Ik Joon's younger sister, enjoy a rare date while eating an explosively hot version of spicy noodles in black bean sauce. Cool and calm Joon Wan mixes the noodles for Ik Soon, showing a warmer side of himself.

Everett Collection/アフロ

Enjoy Watching K-dramas with an Authentic Korean Cocktail!

There's nothing better than relaxing with a drink while watching your favorite K-drama. Why not do it Korean style with these great soju- and makgeolli-based cocktail recipes?

No. 1
Yakult Sorbet Soju

No. 2
Yuzu Makgeolli

No. 3
Goldfish Soju

No. 4
Hot Makgeolli

No. 5
Korean Mojito

No. 6
Kahlúa Makgeolli

No. 1
Yakult Sorbet Soju

Serves 1

**2 bottles Yakult (100 ml each) or
similar yogurt drink**
⅓ cup (80 ml) soju

Freeze the Yakult and soju in ice-cube trays. When frozen, put the cubes in a blender and blend until you have a sorbet consistency. Pour into a chilled glass.

No. 2
Yuzu Makgeolli

Serves 1

¾ cup (200 ml) makgeolli
**3½ tablespoons clear lemon-lime
soda (e.g., Sprite)**
1 tablespoon yuja tea

Combine all the ingredients and pour into a glass.

No. 3
Goldfish Soju

Serves 1

Ice cubes
6½ tablespoons soju
6½ tablespoons water
2 perilla leaves, ripped up
1 small red chili pepper

Put the ice cubes in a glass, and pour in the soju and water. Add the perilla leaves and chili pepper.

No. 4
Hot Makgeolli

Serves 1

¼ Asian pear
1 cup (240 ml) makgeolli
1 cinnamon stick
2 dried red dates
2 black peppercorns

Slice the pear with the peel on. Put all the ingredients in a pan over medium heat. When the pan comes to a boil turn the heat to low and simmer for 5–10 minutes. This is also delicious with ginger, cloves and other spices!

No. 5
Korean Mojito

Serves 1

1 lime
1 tablespoon brown sugar
10 perilla leaves, ripped up
Ice cubes
3½ tablespoons soju
3½ tablespoons soda water

Cut the lime into quarters. Put the lime and brown sugar into a glass, and dissolve the sugar while crushing the lime. Add the perilla leaves and crush, then add the ice cubes, soju and soda water in that order. Mix well.

No. 6
Kahlúa Makgeolli

Serves 1

1 teaspoon instant coffee
1 tablespoon boiling water
1 teaspoon sugar
1 teaspoon condensed milk
½ cup (120 ml) makgeolli
Ice cubes

Mix the coffee with the boiling water. When the coffee granules have dissolved, add the sugar and condensed milk, mix and pour into a glass. Add the makgeolli and ice cubes.

Chapter 3

Delicious Korean Noodles, Rice and Snacks

Chicken Noodle Soup Dal Kalguksu 칼국수

Serves 2
PREPARATION TIME: 40 minutes

6 cups (1.5 L) water
1 large boneless chicken breast,
 about ½ pound (250 g)
½ zucchini
7 oz (200 g) dried kalguksu
 noodles
1 teaspoon chicken soup stock
 granules
Dadaegi Spicy Meat Sauce, to
 taste (see page 115)

SEASONING MIX
1 teaspoon salt
1 teaspoon sesame oil
1 teaspoon finely minced green
 onion
Pepper, to taste

1 Put the 6 cups of water and the chicken breast in a pan over high heat. When the pan comes to a boil, turn the heat to medium and simmer for 20 minutes while skimming off the scum. When the chicken is cooked through and tender, take it out. Reserve the liquid. Shred the chicken with your hands while it's still warm.

2 Divide the Step 1 chicken into two bowls. Combine the Seasoning Mix ingredients and divide evenly between the two bowls.

3 Cut the zucchini into thin matchsticks.

4 Boil the noodles until they are cooked through but still firm.

5 Put the chicken soup stock granules into the reserved liquid from Step 1 and re-heat. When the pan comes back to a boil add the zucchini and the noodles, and simmer for about a minute.

6 Distribute the soup and noodles into the bowls. Add Dadaegi Spicy Meat Sauce to taste.

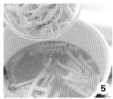

Note Kalguksu means "knife-cut wheat noodles," and you'll find a lot of kalgusu restaurants In South Korea. There are many different kalgusu dishes, including ones made with clams or meat, but this chicken version is the easiest to make.

The Noodle Soup in Episode 2 of *Hospital Playlist*

The five doctors have dinner at a noodle soup restaurant after work. Their personalities clash with each other and they can't agree on anything. They even argue over what to have to end the meal. Finally Seok Hyung brings them all together.

Everett Collection/アフロ

Mussels with Spicy Noodle Soup

Jjamppong 홍합짬뽕

Serves 2
PREPARATION TIME: 40 minutes

½ onion
1 large green onion
2 leaves napa cabbage
4 oz (110 g) thinly sliced pork belly
12 oz (350 g) mussels
2 tablespoons vegetable oil
2½ cups (600 ml) water
2 baby bok choy
2 servings dried Chinese egg noodles, about 4 oz (120 g) per serving

SEASONING MIX
1 tablespoon chili pepper powder
1½ tablespoons soy sauce
1 tablespoon chili oil
1 tablespoon light soy sauce
½ teaspoon salt
½ teaspoon pepper

1 Cut the onion into ½ inch (1 cm) thick slices. Cut the green onion into 2 inch (5 cm) long pieces. Cut the napa cabbage into 1 inch (3 cm) wide strips. Cut the pork belly into ¾ inch (2 cm) wide pieces. Remove the beards from the mussels, wash well under running water, and drain in a colander.

2 Combine the Seasoning Mix ingredients.

3 Put the vegetable oil in a frying pan over high heat. Stir-fry the onion and green onion until lightly browned and fragrant. Add the pork belly and stir-fry over medium heat for 2 minutes. Add the Seasoning Mix ingredients.

4 Put the 2½ cups of water and the bok choy, napa cabbage and mussels into the frying pan and turn the heat to high. When the pan comes to a boil lower the heat to medium, and simmer for about 5 minutes.

5 Cook the Chinese egg noodles following the instructions on the packet and drain well. Divide between two bowls. Ladle in the mussel soup into the bowls.

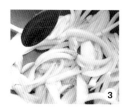

Note When chili pepper powder is stir-fried, this lessens its "raw" flavor and makes it really tasty. If you don't have mussels, this soup works well with squid or other seafood.

The Mussels with Spicy Noodle Soup in Episode 8 of *It's Okay to Not Be Okay*

This soup is a favorite dish of Gang Tae and his siblings, packed with memories of their mother, and when Gang Tae takes Moon Young to have some, he can't help crying. Moon Young can't believe how spicy it is, but manages to finish it all.

Everett Collection/アフロ

Clam Congee Bajilag Juk 바지락죽

Serves 2
PREPARATION TIME: 20 minutes (after soaking the rice)

¾ cup (150 g) uncooked medium grain rice
Water for soaking
1 cup (150 g) shucked Manila clams or other small clams
¼ carrot
¼ onion
¼ zucchini
2 mushrooms
Green onion, for garnish
1 tablespoon sesame oil
3½ cups (800 ml) water
Salt, to taste

1 Wash the rice, soak it in water for 30 minutes, and drain into a colander.

2 Rinse the shelled clams and drain into a colander.

3 Cut the carrot, onion, zucchini and mushrooms into ¼ inch (5 mm) dice. Slice the green onion thinly.

4 Heat the sesame oil in a pan. Add the drained rice and clams and stir-fry. When the rice is translucent add the carrots and continue stir-frying.

5 Add the 3½ cups of water and turn the heat to high. When the water comes to a boil, add the onion, zucchini and mushroom. Simmer over medium-low heat for about 15 minutes until the rice is cooked through, stirring it up occasionally so that it does not burn. Keep simmering until it is thickened.

6 Ladle into bowls and top with the green onions. Add salt to taste.

Note This type of congee is easy to digest and very nutritious, and is often eaten as a healthy breakfast in Asia. Stir-frying the rice with sesame oil makes this dish fragrant and rich. If you add salt during the cooking process, the congee will not thicken well, so add it just before eating.

The Clam Congee in Episode 9 of *Chocolate*

This takes place in the kitchen of the hospice where Kang and Cha Yeong work. They make clam congee, aided by one of the staff, who has Alzheimer's, but can remember each of the recipe steps for this dish.

Ox Bone Soup Seolleongtang 설렁탕

Serves 4
PREPARATION TIME: at least 6 hours

2¼ lbs (1 kg) oxtail or beef marrow bones, cut up
1 lb (450 g) piece beef shank
Water for soaking
8 cups (2 L) water
2 large green onions
5 garlic cloves, peeled
Small piece ginger, roughly chopped
5 black peppercorns
7 oz (200 g) dried somyeon or somen noodles
Salt and pepper, to taste

1 Wash the oxtail or beef marrow bones and beef shank well, and put into separate bowls. Soak each in water to get rid of the blood for about an hour, changing the water several times in the process. Drain both well.

2 Put the 8 cups of water, oxtail or beef marrow bones and beef shank in a large pot. Add the green parts of the green onions (reserving the whites for Step 6), garlic cloves, roughly chopped ginger and peppercorns. Heat over high heat.

3 When the water comes to a boil skim off the scum and lower the heat to medium-low. Gently boil for at least 5 hours, adding more water if it boils down too low.

4 Cook the noodles in a separate pot. Rinse under running water and drain well.

5 Remove the beef shank from the pot and cut into ¼ inch (5mm) dice. Put the noodles, oxtail or marrow bone and beef shank into bowls, and ladle in the soup.

6 Slice the remaining green onion, and add to each bowl as a garnish. Season with salt and pepper.

Note Ox bone soup is a usually cooked for several days while adding water to the pot. It takes some time until the umami in the beef has melted out and the soup becomes milky white, but you just need to keep it boiling. I hope you give it a try!

The Ox Bone Soup in Episode 3 of *She Was Pretty*

After getting drunk and injured, Ha-ri and Sung-joon stop by a restaurant that serves ox bone soup on their way back from the hospital. Sung-joon, who thinks that Ha-ri is his first love Hye-jin, talks about the memories he has of his late mother with a gentle expression that he does not show at work.

Everett Collection/アフロ

Hand-torn Noodle Soup Sujebi 수제비

Serves 2
PREPARATION TIME: 1 hour

½ zucchini
1 potato
1 large green onion
4¼ cups (1 L) dried anchovy
    stock (see page 35)
1 cup (50 g) dried shrimp
1 teaspoon salted anchovy
    extract, or light soy sauce
All-purpose Korean-style Soy
    Sauce (see page 108), to taste

FOR THE NOODLE DOUGH
1 potato
1¾ cups (200 g) flour
1 teaspoon vegetable oil
½ teaspoon salt
Water, to mix

1 To make the dough, start by peeling and grating the potato. Put the flour, the grated potato, vegetable oil and salt in a bowl. Knead into a dough while adding water little by little. When the dough is smooth and shiny and does not stick to your hands, form into a ball, wrap in cling film and refrigerate for 30 minutes.

2 Cut the zucchini in half lengthwise and cut into ½ inch (1 cm) thick slices. Peel and halve the potato and cut into ¼ inch (5 mm) thick slices. Cut the green onion into diagonal slices.

3 Put the anchovy stock in a pan over high heat. When the stock comes to a boil add the Step 2 potato. Tear off small pieces of the dough and stretch the pieces out thinly with moistened hands and put into the pan.

4 When the dough floats to the surface of the soup, add the zucchini, dried shrimp and salted anchovy extract. Simmer for about 3 minutes.

5 Ladle into bowls, and add the All-purpose Korean-style Soy Sauce to taste.

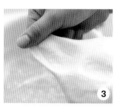

Note This soup is made with bits of dough, rather like pot noodles, that are simmered in a broth made with meat or seafood. It's a very old home-cooked dish, with a simple and satisfying flavor.

The Hand-torn Noodle Soup in Episode 5 of *One Spring Night*

Jung-in goes to Ji Ho's home to ask him if she's being a nuisance. Ji Ho takes the crying Jung-in to a restaurant he goes to all the time. There, Jung-in tells Ji Ho to eat the hand-torn noodle soup, which she also wants to eat.

Pine-nut Noodles Jat-guksu 잣국수

Serves 2
PREPARATION TIME: 20 minutes

¼ zucchini
1 dried shiitake mushroom
6 oz (180 g) dried kalguksu
noodles
1 cup (150 g) pine nuts
2 cups (480 ml) water
Coarse salt, to taste

1 Cut the zucchini into thin matchsticks. Soak the shiitake mushroom to rehydrate it, and slice thinly.

2 Boil the noodles until they are cooked through but still on the firm side. Drain in a colander.

3 Blend the pine nuts and the 2 cups of water in a blender or food processor until smooth. Transfer to a pan and heat over high heat.

4 When the pan comes to a boil lower the heat to medium. Add the noodles, the zucchini and the shiitake, and bring back to a boil. Season with coarse salt to taste.

Note Since the soup won't become creamy if you add salt, season it just before eating. In the drama this was a hot soup, but in the summer this pine nut noodle soup is delicious served chilled and topped with shredded cucumber.

The Pine-nut Noodles in Episode 8 of *Start-Up*

On Ji Pyung's birthday, Dal Mi gives him a gift set containing the ingredients to make the famous pine-nut noodles from a certain country town. Ji Pyung considers it a bother but tries making it anyway, and is amazed at how delicious it is!

Everett Collection/アフロ

Beef Soup Gukbap 국밥

Serves 4
PREPARATION TIME: 30 minutes

½ head napa cabbage
7 oz (200 g) thinly sliced beef
2 tablespoons grated garlic
4 tablespoons doenjang soybean paste, or red miso paste
6 cups (1.5 L) water
1 large green onion
1 tablespoon anchovy powder (see Note)
2 tablespoons chili pepper powder
1 tablespoon coarse salt
1 tablespoon salted anchovy extract, or Thai fish sauce

1 Rip off the napa cabbage leaves from the root end. Blanch them in boiling water, rinse and squeeze out. Cut into bite-sized pieces. Cut the beef into bite-sized pieces.

2 Transfer the napa cabbage and beef to a bowl. Add the grated garlic and doenjang, and rub and squeeze them in with your hands.

3 Put the water, napa cabbage and beef in a pan over high heat. When the pan comes to a boil, lower the heat to medium. Slice the green onion diagonally and add to the pan with the anchovy powder and chili pepper powder. Bring the pan back to a boil.

4 Season with coarse salt and salted anchovy extract to finish.

Note Anchovy powder is available at Korean grocery stores. Alternatively, grind up dried anchovies in a food processor. Since anchovy powder instantly adds umami, you can skip the step of making stock for the soup.

The Beef Soup in Episode 3 of *Something in the Rain*

Jin-Ah sees Joon Hee go out to eat with a female coworker and feels rather upset. In order to distract herself, she goes out to have beef soup with a younger coworker and is talking about love and relationships with her when she gets a call from an ex-boyfriend . . .

Everett Collection/アフロ

Kimbap Sushi Rolls Gimbap 김밥

Makes 4 rolls
PREPARATION TIME: 1 hour

FILLING 1: OMELET
4 eggs

SEASONING MIX A
1 teaspoon grated garlic
1 teaspoon mirin
Pinch of salt

FILLING 2: CARROT NAMUL
Vegetable oil, for frying
1 carrot, shredded

SEASONING MIX B
1 teaspoon grated garlic
1 teaspoon salt

FILLING 3: SPINACH NAMUL
1 bunch spinach, 7 oz (200 g)

SEASONING MIX C
1 teaspoon grated garlic
1 teaspoon salt
1 teaspoon sesame oil

FILLING 4: GROUND BEEF
7 oz (200 g) ground beef

SEASONING MIX D
1½ tablespoons soy sauce
½ tablespoon sugar
1 teaspoon grated garlic
1 teaspoon sesame oil
Pepper

FILLING 5: FISH CAKES
7 oz (200 g) eomuk fish cakes

SEASONING MIX E
1½ tablespoons soy sauce
½ tablespoon sugar
1 teaspoon grated garlic
1 teaspoon sesame oil
Pepper

FILLING 6: PICKLED RADISH
4 oz (110 g) pickled daikon radish
(danmuji)

SEASONING MIX F
1 tablespoon sesame oil
½ teaspoon salt
1 tablespoon roasted sesame
seeds

3¾ cups (750 g) warm cooked
rice
4 sheets gim or nori seaweed
A little sesame oil
Roasted sesame seeds, for
garnish

Note To make this a bit easier, use canned luncheon meat instead of the ground beef. Try various fillings, depending on what you like. This is a standard item in packed lunches at sports festivals or for school outings in South Korea, but unlike Japanese sushi rolls the rice does not contain any vinegar and can spoil easily in the summer, so watch out for that.

The Kimbap in Episode 13 of *She Was Pretty*

Seo-joon and Hye-jin come to the office on a Sunday when no one else is there. They go for a two-hour lunch break in the park. They eat the kimbap packed lunch that Hye-jin made, and Seo-joon says that when he's become successful in his job, he wants to propose to her.

Everett Collection/アフロ

1 ~ 6

1 Make Filling 1: the omelet. Combine the eggs and Seasoning Mix A in a bowl and beat well. Make the omelet in a frying pan, and cut into 4 pieces lengthwise.

2 Make Filling 2: carrot namul. Put the vegetable oil in a heated frying pan with the shredded carrot and Seasoning Mix B. Stir-fry over medium heat.

3 Make Filling 3: spinach namul. Boil the spinach briefly, cool in cold water and squeeze out well. Mix with Seasoning Mix C.

4 Make Filling 4: the ground beef. Stir-fry the beef in an unoiled frying pan over medium heat. When it changes color add Seasoning Mix D, and cook until the liquid is almost gone.

5 Make Filling 5: the fish cakes. Cut the fish cakes into ½ inch (1cm) wide strips and stir-fry in an unoiled frying pan over medium heat. Add Seasoning Mix E, and cook until the liquid is almost gone.

6 Make Filling 6: the pickled radish. Drain the pickled daikon radish, cut in half lengthwise and slice thinly.

7 Add Seasoning Mix F to the warm rice and cut it in. Place a sheet of gim or nori seaweed on a sushi rolling mat. Leave a ½ inch (1 cm) gap at the far end of the sheet of seaweed and spread out a quarter of the rice mixture evenly.

8 Place a quarter of each of the fillings in the center of the rice as shown in photo 8, opposite. Roll it up tightly. Make 3 more rolls in the same way.

9 Brush the surface of the seaweed with sesame oil and sprinkle with sesame seeds. Cut into ⅔ inch (1.5 cm) thick slices. Arrange with the cut sides up.

Seen All The Time in K-dramas! Recipes Using Instant Ramyeon Noodles

No. 1 Cheesy Chicken Ramyeon

A soupless ramyeon where the noodles are mixed with creamy melted cheese, chicken and spices. It has a lot going on and is deliciously juicy and meaty.

No. 2 Carbonara Ramyeon

A very well-seasoned carbonara-style noodle dish. This version is spicy to appeal to grown-ups. You can adjust the spiciness with the amount of spicy soup powder you use!

Instant ramyeon or ramen noodles always appear in K-dramas. Here I show you some recipes that turn an everyday snack into something special.

No. 3 Spicy Beef Soup Ramyeon

In South Korea the spicy beef soup called yukgaejang, is often eaten as a hangover cure. What makes this dish delicious are the meat juices.

No. 4 Ramyeon Pancakes

Drain the noodles well before pan-frying them for a really crispy finish. Or, leave them a little moist for a bouncy texture. Either way, cook this pancake with a generous amount of oil.

Cheesy Chicken Ramyeon

Serves 1
PREPARATION TIME: 20 minutes

1–2 boneless chicken thighs,
   about 5 oz (150 g)
2 cabbage leaves
¼ onion
2 perilla leaves
1 tablespoon vegetable oil
1 packet spicy instant ramyeon
   or ramen noodles
4 teaspoons sesame oil
2 tbsps shredded pizza cheese

SEASONING MIX

1½ tablespoons gochujang paste
½ tablespoon sugar
1 tablespoon soy sauce
1 teaspoon grated garlic
1 tablespoon honey
½ packet ramyeon soup powder
   (from the instant ramyeon pkt)

1 Cut the chicken into bite-sized pieces. Roughly chop the cabbage and onion. Chop the perilla leaves. Combine the Seasoning Mix ingredients in a bowl.

2 Put the vegetable oil in a frying pan and stir-fry the chicken. When the chicken is cooked through, add the combined Seasoning Mix ingredients and mix. Add the cabbage and onion and stir-fry quickly.

3 Boil the noodles for 4 minutes and drain into a colander. Transfer to a bowl, mix with the sesame oil and then arrange on your serving plate.

4 Put the stir-fried chicken and vegetables over the noodles and top with the pizza cheese. Garnish with the chopped perilla leaves.

Carbonara Ramyeon

Serves 1
PREPARATION TIME: 15 minutes

¼ onion
2 mushrooms
2 garlic cloves
3 slices bacon
1 packet spicy instant ramyeon
   or ramen noodles
1 tablespoon butter
1 cup (240 ml) heavy cream
1 slice processed cheese
½ packet ramyeon soup powder
   (from the instant ramyeon pkt)
Green onion, chopped, for
   garnish

1 Slice the onion thinly. Cut the mushrooms into thirds. Slice the garlic. Cut the bacon into ¾ inch (2 cm) wide pieces.

2 Boil the noodles for 2 minutes and drain into a colander.

3 Melt the butter in a frying pan, add all the Step 1 ingredients and stir-fry. When the onion is translucent, add the heavy cream and the slice of cheese, then add the soup powder and mix.

4 When the cheese has melted, add the noodles to the pan and simmer for another 2 minutes. Arrange on a plate and garnish with green onion.

Spicy Beef Soup Ramyeon

Serves 1
PREPARATION TIME: 20 minutes

1 large green onion
4 oz (110 g) thinly sliced beef
1 tablespoon vegetable oil
2¼ cups (550 ml) water
1 packet instant ramyeon or
   ramen noodles
½ cup (60 g) bean sprouts

SEASONING MIX
1 tablespoon chili pepper
   powder
1 tablespoon soy sauce
Pepper

1 Slice the green onion thinly. Cut the beef into 1.5 inch (4 cm) wide pieces.

2 Put the beef and green onion in a bowl and combine with the Seasoning Mix ingredients.

3 Put the vegetable oil in a frying pan. Add the Step 2 ingredients and stir-fry. When the meat changes color, add the water. Bring to a boil, add the noodles and simmer for about 5 minutes.

4 Turn off the heat, add the bean sprouts, mix quickly and serve.

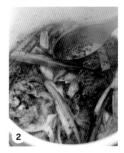

Ramyeon Pancakes

Serves 1
PREPARATION TIME: 20 minutes

1 large green onion
2 slices bacon
1 packet spicy instant ramyeon
   or ramen noodles
½ packet ramyeon soup powder
   (from the instant ramyeon pkt)
3 tablespoons vegetable oil

1 Chop the green onion. Cut the bacon into ¾ inch (2 cm) pieces.

2 Boil the noodles for about 2 minutes and drain into a colander. Transfer to a bowl and add the green onion and bacon, plus the soup powder. Mix well.

3 Put the vegetable oil in a frying pan and heat. When it is hot lower the heat to medium, spread the oil around the pan and spread the Step 2 mixture around it thinly. Shallow-fry the noodles until the pancake is browned and crispy on both sides.

Snacks to Nibble While Watching Your Favorite K-dramas

If you like to unwind with a drink while watching your favorite K-drama, you're probably not alone! Why not try some of the delicious cocktails on page 56, along with some of the tasty Korean-style drinking snacks on the following pages?

Spicy Whelks  Golbaengi-muchim 골뱅이무침

Serves 2
PREPARATION TIME: 20 minutes

1 can whelks, about 7 oz (200 g), or 7 oz (200 g) clams
Small bunch water celery, about 2 oz (60 g)
½ onion
½ small Japanese cucumber
Roasted sesame seeds, for garnish

SEASONING MIX
3 tablespoons chili pepper powder
3 tablespoons green plum extract, or 1½ tablespoons sugar
3 tablespoons soy sauce
1 tablespoon vinegar
2 tablespoons whelk can juices
1 teaspoon sesame oil

Note Whelks (golbaengi) are a type of sea snail, available canned in Korean groceries. If you can't get hold of whelks, this dish also works well with other seafood, such as shrimp, mussels or clams.

1 Drain the canned whelks into a colander, and cut into bite-sized pieces.

2 Wash the water celery well, and cut into 2 inch (5 cm) long pieces. Slice the onion thinly. Cut the cucumber in half then slice diagonally.

3 Put the Seasoning Mix ingredients in a bowl and mix.

4 Add all the other ingredients to the bowl and arrange on a plate. Sprinkle with sesame seeds to finish.

French Fries with Dadaegi Sauce

Serves 2
PREPARATION TIME: 20 minutes

12 oz (350 g) frozen french fries
½ cup (120 g) Dadaegi Spicy
**   Meat Sauce (see page 115)**
2 slices processed cheese
Pepper, to taste

1 Cook the french fries following the instructions on the packet.

2 Put the french fries on a plate, top with the dadaegi and cheese, and season with the pepper.

Note The sweetness of the french fries, the spiciness of the dadaegi and the richness of the cheese marry together perfectly. This popular dish is often served at parties.

Crudités with Gochujang Dip

Serves 2
PREPARATION TIME: 10 minutes

1 small or ½ large cucumber
¼ daikon radish, about 4 oz (110 g)
½ carrot

FOR THE DIP
1 tablespoon gochujang paste
1 tablespoon peanut butter
2 tablespoons light corn syrup
1 teaspoon sesame oil
1 tablespoon chopped nuts

1 Cut off both ends of the cucumber, and then cut into sticks.

2 Peel the daikon radish and carrot and cut into sticks.

3 Make the dip. Put all the dip ingredients in a bowl and mix well.

4 Serve the vegetable sticks with the dip.

Note Bell peppers and celery go well with this dip too. It's perfect as a drinking snack, but if you serve it to children, you may want to adjust the amount of gochujang you use.

Boiled Squid with Chili Sauce

Serves 1
PREPARATION TIME: 15 minutes

1 fresh squid
½ tablespoon salt
1 tablespoon sake or cheongju

FOR THE SPICY DIPPING SAUCE
1 tablespoon gochujang paste
1 tablespoon rice vinegar
1 tablespoon sugar
½ tablespoon chili pepper powder
1 teaspoon grated garlic
1 teaspoon sesame oil

1 Clean the squid. Put the squid, salt and sake in a pan of boiling water, and boil the squid for 2 minutes. Drain into a colander.

2 Combine the sauce ingredients in a bowl.

3 Cut the squid into easy-to-eat pieces and arrange on a plate. Serve with the dipping sauce on the side.

Note In South Korea, sashimi is also eaten with this spicy dipping sauce rather than soy sauce. It is also delicious with vegetables or seaweed, so you could make a larger quantity to have on hand.

Persimmon, Cream Cheese and Walnut Rolls

Serves 2
PREPARATION TIME: 15 minutes
(not including chilling time)

4 dried persimmons
4 oz (110 g) cream cheese
4 walnuts

1 Remove the calyxes from the persimmons. Slice the persimmons in the middle, open them up and take out the pits.

2 Place the opened persimmons on cling film, and flatten them with a rolling pin. Spread each persimmon evenly with the cream cheese, and top with the walnuts.

3 Roll up each persimmon inside a piece of cling film, and wrap up like pieces of candy.

4 Refrigerate for 20 minutes. Slice and serve.

Note Soft cream cheese is easier to slice if you chill it first. The combination of sweet persimmon and salty cheese is quite addictive. This is a great accompaniment to a glass of wine!

Chapter 4

Homemade Kimchi and Comforting Hot Pots

Why Not Try Making Kimchi on the Weekend?

Kimchi almost always appears in K-dramas. It's easy to buy readymade kimchi, but if you're a K-drama aficionado, why not trying making it yourself at least once? It is delicious, you know exactly what goes in it, and you can use it in a lot of recipes so it ends up being quite economical. Make a ton of it when you have the time, by following the three easy steps on these pages.

1 Make salt-pickled napa cabbage

1 cup (300 g) coarse salt
13 cups (3 L) water
1 head napa cabbage

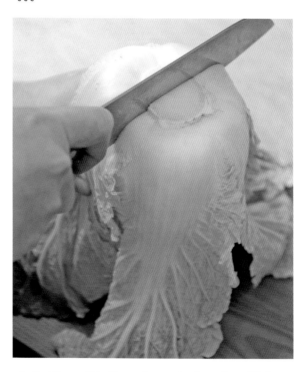

1 Put the salt in the water and mix well until it is dissolved. Take off the wilted outer leaves of the napa cabbage (keep in reserve). Make a crisscross cut in the root end of the cabbage, and split the cabbage into 4 pieces.

2 Put the quartered cabbage in the salt water with the cut sides facing down for 2 hours. Turn the cabbage pieces over after 2 hours, and leave for another 2 hours.

3 When pickling the cabbage pieces in the salt water, use the reserved outer leaves as lids to keep the cabbage in the dark. These outer leaves will be used later too, so don't throw them away.

4 After 4 hours, fold back a thick part of the cabbage. If it doesn't break and simply bends, the cabbage is pickled well. If it doesn't bend easily, leave to pickle for longer.

5 When pickled, rinse the cabbage under running water. Put the pieces on a flat sieve or colander with the cut sides down so they drain well, and leave to drain for at least 1 hour.

2 Make the kimchi sauce

FOR 1 HEAD OF NAPA CABBAGE
2¼ lbs (1 kg) daikon radish, shredded
3–4 large green onions, about 4 oz (110 g), cut into
  2 inch (5 cm) lengths
7 tablespoons chili pepper powder

SEASONING MIX
5 tablespoons salted anchovy extract
2½ oz (75 g) salted shrimp
2 oz (50 g) grated garlic
Small piece ginger
½ cup (80 g) cold cooked rice
1½ tablespoons sugar
1½ tablespoons green plum extract, or a further
  1½ tablespoons sugar

Note There are no good substitutes for salted anchovy extract or salted shrimp here. Be sure to buy in advance.

1 Combine all the Seasoning Mix ingredients in a blender or food processor.

2 Put the shredded daikon radish and cut green onion in a large bowl. Sprinkle in the chili pepper powder, and add the Step 1 ingredients.

3 Mix everything up and leave for about 10 minutes.

3 Pickle the napa cabbage in the kimchi sauce

1 Put the pickled cabbage pieces cut side up in a container with a lid. Cover the cabbage leaves in the kimchi sauce, starting at the root ends.

2 When you close the leaves back up, the kimchi sauce should spread to cover. Take care not to let the kimchi sauce fall out.

3 Place the reserved outer leaves of the cabbage on top of the container to shut out the air (if you don't have them you can use cling film instead).

Done!

4 Cover the container with the lid, and let it sit at room temperature for 2 to 3 days to mature. Transfer to the refrigerator. For sour mature kimchi let it sit at room temperature until it tastes sour.

Daikon Radish Kimchi Kkakdugi 깍두기

Serves 2
PREPARATION TIME: 90 minutes
(including pickling)

1 large daikon radish, about 1½
lbs (680 g)
1 tablespoon coarse salt
1 bottle Yakult or similar yogurt
drink
2 large green onions, about 2 oz
(60 g)
7 oz (200 g) kimchi sauce (see
page 88)

1 Cut the daikon radish into ¾ inch (2 cm) dice. Put into a bowl with the salt and Yakult, and leave for about 1 hour.

2 Cut the green onions into pieces about 2 inches (5 cm) long.

3 Put the daikon radish in a colander and drain well. Transfer to a bowl. Add the kimchi sauce and green onion and mix.

Note Since daikon radish can sometimes contain a lot of water, draining off the excess moisture in Step 3 is very important. By removing this excess moisture, you end up with very crunchy daikon radish kimchi.

Cucumber Kimchi Oi Kimchi 오이김치

Serves 2
PREPARATION TIME: 2½ hours
(including salting)

5 small Japanese cucumbers or
  pickling cucumbers
2 tablespoons coarse salt
2 oz (60 g) garlic chives
4 oz (110 g) kimchi sauce (see
  page 88)

1 Cut the cucumbers into thirds. Make deep crisscross cuts into each third, leaving the ends intact. Sprinkle with the salt and rub it in well. Leave for 2 hours, then drain in a colander.

2 Cut the garlic chives into ¾ inch (2 cm) long pieces.

3 Combine the kimchi sauce and garlic chives, and stuff it into the cut parts of the cucumber pieces.

Note For an easy version, cut the cucumber into bite-sized pieces and mix with the chopped garlic chives and kimchi sauce. It will still be delicious.

Yam and Apple Kimchi Masagwa Kimchi 마사과김치

Serves 2
PREPARATION TIME: 10 minutes

½ pound (250 g) Chinese yam, or
   pears
½ apple
3 green onions
2 tablespoons kimchi sauce (see
   page 88)
1 teaspoon green plum extract,
   or 1 teaspoon sugar

1 Peel the yam and apple and cut into thin matchsticks. Cut the green onions into ½ inch (1 cm) pieces.

2 Put the vegetables in a bowl, and mix with the kimchi sauce and green plum extract. Refrigerate it for a while to let the flavors penetrate.

Note Pears or unripe persimmons also work well in this recipe. Try it with any seasonal produce that is easy for you to come by.

Kimchi Fried Rice Kimchi Bokkeumbap 김치볶음밥

Serves 2
PREPARATION TIME: 15 minutes

⅔ cup (100 g) mature sour
   kimchi
1 teaspoon gochujang paste
1 teaspoon sugar
2 strips bacon or 2 slices of
   canned luncheon meat
1½ cups (300 g) cold cooked rice
¾ tablespoon butter
2 eggs and oil for frying
Shredded gim or nori seaweed,
   for garnish
Sesame seeds, for garnish

1 Squeeze out the mature kimchi lightly, and season with the gochujang and sugar.

2 Cut the bacon into ⅓ inch (1 cm) pieces. Heat a frying pan, set the heat to medium and stir-fry the bacon. Add the kimchi to the pan.

3 Put the cold rice in the frying pan and stir-fry.

4 Add the butter and mix in. Turn off the heat and arrange on plates.

5 Fry the eggs and use them to top each serving. Garnish with the seaweed and sesame seeds.

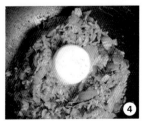

Note In South Korea, year-old kimchi is often used for this. Mature kimchi can be quite sour, so if you season it with gochujang and sugar to add sweetness, the sourness will be lessened.

Kimchi Hot Pot  Kimchi Jjigae 김치찌개

Serves 4
PREPARATION TIME: 90 minutes

1 lb (450 g) pork spare ribs
Water for soaking and rinsing
4 cups (600 g) mature kimchi
2 cups (480 ml) water
2 large green onions
1 tablespoon salted shrimp
1 block firm tofu, about 14 oz
  (400 g)

SEASONING MIX A
1 tablespoon doenjang soybean
  paste, or red miso paste
1 teaspoon instant coffee
Green part of 2 large green
  onions
2 cups (480 ml) water

SEASONING MIX B
1 tablespoon vegetable oil
1 tablespoon sesame oil
½ tablespoon sugar
1 tablespoon mirim or mirin
1 tablespoon chili pepper
  powder

1 Soak the spare ribs for at least 30 minutes in water to drain out the blood.

2 Drain off the soaking water and put the spare ribs in a pan with the combined Seasoning Mix A ingredients. Bring to a boil. Cook for 5 minutes.

3 Drain the spare ribs and rinse them with water. Drain again.

4 Drain off the kimchi lightly, reserving the drained-off liquid (see Note, below), and cut into 2 inch (5 cm) pieces.

5 Cut up the kimchi and add it to a pan with the combined Seasoning Mix B ingredients, and stir-fry over high heat. Add the 2 cups of water to the pan and cook over high heat for 10 minutes.

6 Slice the green onions diagonally. Add the spare ribs, green onions and salted shrimp to the Step 5 pan. Cover the pan with a lid and simmer over medium heat for at least 30 minutes. Slice the tofu, add to the pan, and simmer over low heat for 5 minutes. Sprinkle with the green onions.

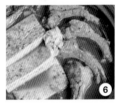

Note Seafood is usually used in Kimchi Hot Pot, but here I have made it with spare ribs. It's a very substantial dish that's a bit different from the usual. If you think it needs a bit more flavor when tasting it, add some of the reserved kimchi liquid for more umami.

The Kimchi Hot Pot in Episode 1 of *Itaewon Class*

Sae Ro Yi is thrown out of his new high school after just one day. His father takes him to a bar-restaurant, where he teaches Sae Ro Yi how to enjoy drinks while they eat kimchi hot pot.

ALBUM/アフロ

Ramyeon Hot Pot with Spicy Rice Cakes

Rabokki 라볶이

Serves 4
PREPARATION TIME: 30 minutes

**1 packet spicy rice cakes
   (tteokbokki), about 7 oz (200 g)
3 square eomuk fish cakes
2 cabbage leaves
½ onion
2 large green onions
Perilla leaves, to taste 1¼ cups
   (300 ml) water
1 packet instant ramyeon or
   ramen noodles
1 hard-boiled egg**

SEASONING MIX
**2 tablespoons gochujang paste
2 tablespoons sugar
2 tablespoons soy sauce
1 tablespoon chili pepper
   powder
1 teaspoon salt**

1 Boil the rice cakes for about 10 minutes to soften them. Combine the Seasoning Mix ingredients.

2 Cut the fish cakes into thirds. Roughly chop the cabbage and slice the onion thinly. Cut the green onions diagonally. Shred the perilla leaves.

3 Put the vegetables in a large, shallow pan. Top with the rice cakes and fish cakes. Pour the combined Seasoning Mix ingredients into the center. Add the water and heat over high heat. When the rice cakes are soft, turn the heat down to medium.

4 Break the block of instant noodles in half and put both halves in the pan. Bring to a boil. Turn off the heat and top with the boiled egg and perilla leaves.

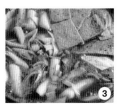

Note If you like spicy food, increase the amount of chili pepper powder. The South Korean way is to add rice to the leftover broth with shredded nori seaweed or gim and sesame oil to turn it into fried rice.

The Ramyeon Hot Pot in Episode 3 of *Record of Youth*

Jeong Ha, who rarely leaves the house, goes to have rabokki with Hye Jun. Jeong Ha exclaims that "ramyeon hot pot with spicy rice cakes is soul food" and gets so excited she starts coughing. Hye Jun pats her on the back.

Everett Collection/アフロ

Beef Tripe Hot Pot

Gopchang-jeongol 곱창전골

Serves 4
PREPARATION TIME: 40 minutes

4 oz (110 g) beef shank
3 fresh shiitake mushrooms
½ onion
3 napa cabbage leaves
Handful shimeji mushrooms, about 1 oz (30 g)
A few sprigs of chrysanthemum greens, about 1 oz (30 g)
12 oz (350 g) parboiled beef tripe or beef offal
3½ cups (800 ml) Beef Bone Soup (see page 27)
1 large green onion, sliced
2 oz (50 g) dried glass or cellophane noodles

SEASONING MIX
1 tablespoon chili pepper powder
1½ tablespoons gochujang paste
½ tablespoon doenjang soybean paste, or red miso paste
1½ tablespoons soy sauce
1 tablespoon grated garlic
1 tablespoon mirim or mirin
Pepper

1 Wash the beef shank well and soak it in water to cover for 1 hour to eliminate the blood. Cut into easy-to-eat pieces.

2 Slice the shiitake mushrooms, onion and napa cabbage thinly. Separate the shimeji mushrooms from the base of the cluster. Cut the chrysanthemum greens into 2 inch (5 cm) long pieces.

3 Put the tripe, beef shank and combined Seasoning Mix ingredients in a bowl and mix well.

4 Put the mushrooms, onion and napa cabbage in a pot. Top with the Step 3 mixture and pour in the beef bone soup. Heat over high heat.

5 When the hot pot comes to a boil turn the heat down to medium, and simmer for about 15 minutes. Add the sliced green onion, chrysanthemum greens and noodles. When the noodles are soft the hot pot is ready.

Note Any leftover broth is delicious mixed with rice and sesame oil, as shown in the photograph on the far right.

The Beef Tripe Hot Pot in Episode 3 of *Was It Love?*

Jeong's mother invites Yeon Woo to dinner, and regales him with beef tripe hot pot. When Yeo Woo says that he is looking for a place to live, she says "Why not come live with us?" which surprises Ha Nee, her granddaughter, who is at the dining table with them.

Everett Collection/アフロ

Mandu Dumpling Hot Pot Mandu Jeongol 만두전골

Serves 2 (20 dumplings)
PREPARATION TIME: 1 hour

FOR THE DUMPLINGS
4 oz (110 g) firm tofu
Small bunch garlic chives, about 2 oz (60 g)
2 oz (60 g) dried glass or cellophane noodles
½ cup (60 g) bean sprouts
5½ oz (150 g) ground pork
20 mandu or gyoza dumpling skins

SEASONING MIX
1 teaspoon salt
1 tablespoon grated garlic
1 teaspoon sesame oil
1 teaspoon light soy sauce
Pepper

FOR THE SOUP
3 napa cabbage leaves
1 large green onion
2 oz (60 g) shimeji mushrooms
6 cups (1.5 L) Beef Bone Soup (page 27)
1 teaspoon grated garlic
1 teaspoon salted anchovy extract, or light soy
   sauce

The Mandu Hot Pot in Episode 3 of *Chocolate*

While battling an illness Min Sung wants to eat mandu dumpling hot pot. His ex-girlfriend Cha Yeong manages to anonymously send him some she has made. As soon as he takes one bite, Min Sung's smile makes us realize that he knows only Cha Yeong could have made it.

TO MAKE THE DUMPLINGS

1 Crush the tofu, wrap it in paper towels, and squeeze out the water.

2 Chop the garlic chives finely. Cook the noodles and boil the bean sprouts briefly. Drain and chop the noodles and bean sprouts finely.

3 Put the ground pork, the tofu from Step 1, the Step 2 ingredients and the combined Seasoning Mix ingredients in a bowl and mix well.

4 Put a spoonful of the Step 3 mix in the middle of a dumpling skin. Wet the edges with water, fold in half, and pinch lightly with your fingers. Bring the two edges of the dumplings together and secure them with a little water. Repeat until all the dumpling skins have been filled with the mixture.

TO MAKE THE SOUP

1 Shred the napa cabbage leaves, and slice the green onion diagonally. Separate the shimeji mushrooms from the base of the cluster.

2 Put the cabbage and green onion in a large, shallow pan and top with the dumplings and shimeji mushrooms. Add enough beef bone soup to cover, and heat over high heat. When the pan comes to a boil turn the heat down to medium, add the grated garlic, and simmer until the dumplings are cooked through.

3 Season with the salted anchovy extract.

DUMPLINGS

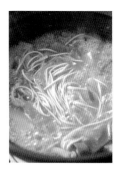

Note Although the dumplings may look hard to make, they are surprisingly simple. They are easy to eat in one mouthful, and fill your mouth with meat juices. If there is any leftover soup after finishing the dumplings, add some thick wheat noodles (like udon). You can also make this dish spicy by adding some Dadaegi Spicy Meat Sauce (see page 115).

DUMPLINGS 4

DUMPLINGS 4

DUMPLINGS 4

SOUP 2

Shopping for Ingredients in Seoul

If you're lucky enough to find yourself in Seoul, let me introduce you to the stores where I love to do my food shopping.

When you have no time to go to the food markets, or when you want to purchase food in small packets that you can use as gifts, I recommend the basement food department at Shinsegae Department Store in Myeong-dong. Here you can buy items that can be hard to find elsewhere such as perilla oil, Korean chili pepper powder, salt-fermented seafood, seaweed, Korean snacks and more, in suitable gift sizes.

Shinsegae Department Store

Address: 63 Sogong-ro, Jung-gu, Seoul, South Korea

Access: Directly connected to the no. 7 exit at Hoehyeon Station on the No. 4 Seoul Subway Line

The items I buy here:

Salted anchovy extract
(myeolchi-jeot)

Salted shrimp
(saeu-jeot)

Perilla oil
(deulgireum)

중부건어물시장
Jungbu Dried Seafoods Market

1문

Jungbu Market

Address: 35 Eulji-ro 36-gil, Ojang-dong, Jung-gu, Seoul, South Korea

Access: 3-min walk from Seoul Subway no. 2 line Euljiro 4-ga Station, exit 7; or a 6-min walk from Dong-daemun History & Culture Park Station no. 5 line, exit 7.

Situated between Myeong-dong and Dongdaemun with great access, this is a treasure trove of food. There are more than a thousand stores along the tiny streets. Although the market is packed with wholesalers from dawn into the morning, in the evening it is full of shoppers who come here to buy food for dinner. The quality is great, and the prices are 20 to 30 percent cheaper than the department stores.

Namsun Sanfe 남산상회

150 meters from exit no. 1

Salted shrimp (Saeu-jeot)

What I often buy here:

Yujo	500 g	W40000
Chujo	500 g	W10000
Salt-fermented octopus	500 g	W8000
Salted spicy pollack roe	500 g	W10000
Pickled perilla leaves	500 g	W5000

There are two types of salted shrimp, yujo and chujo. Although yujo is regarded as the best, it's expensive, so chujo is fine to use in kimchi.

Pusan Sanfe 부산상회

150 meters from exit no. 1, then turn right

Dried anchovies (Mareun-myeolchi)
Dried kelp (Dasima)
Miyeok seaweed (Miyeok)

What I often buy here:

Dried anchovies	1.5 kg	W30000
Dried kelp	400 g	W7000
Miyeok seaweed	350 g	W7000

I go here to buy dried anchovies for the anchovy stock that is indispensable in Korean cuisine, or when I want to buy a large amount of seaweed. It's cheaper here than at department stores, so I recommend it to people who love to cook.

Sageori Myeolchi 사거리멸치

100 meters from exit no. 1, on the left side

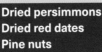

Dried persimmons
Dried red dates
Pine nuts

What I often buy here:

Dried persimmons	7 for	W10000
Dried red dates	300 g	W5000
Pine nuts	500 g	W60000

I can buy good quality dried persimmons here year round, so it's one of the stores I often go to. They also have a large variety of other dried fruits and nuts.

More Korean Ingredients to Up Your Korean Cooking Game!

Oils and seasonings

Try stocking up on these Korean seasonings and other ingredients from your local Korean grocery store or Asian market to make your Korean dishes taste even more authentic.

Perilla oil
Called deulgireum in Korean, this oil has a delicious nutty flavor, and along with sesame oil is a popular seasoning for dishes in Korea. It gives a really authentic flavor to recipes such as Simple Soy-sauce Dressing on page 117.

Light corn syrup
Called mul-yeot in Korean, this light corn syrup is used more often than sugar in Korea. It's light and thin and adds a pleasant sweetness to dishes such as Stir-fried Anchovies (page 125) or Simmered Quail Eggs (page 120).

Even more Korean ingredients

Coarse salt
This is a mild salt with large grains that melt into food slowly, so it's perfect to use when making kimchi. Any kind of coarse salt will work well for the recipes in this book.

Dangmyeon noodles
These noodles are made with sweet potato flour. You can use any kind of glass or cellophane noodles for the recipes in this book, but dangmyeon will give the most authentic results.

Naengmyeon noodles
Also known as Asian vermicelli noodles or buckwheat noodles, these are usually served cold. They are made with buckwheat or soba flour, with potato starch or acorn flour. They are boiled for 1 to 2 minutes and have a unique bouncy texture. Japanese soba noodles are similar but less chewy than the Korean type.

Rice cakes
Called tteok, Korean rice cakes are made with medium-grain rice so they are chewy but not too sticky, and they tend not to fall apart when cooked.

Chapter 5

Korean Flavors in No Time with Tasty Multipurpose Sauces

All-purpose Korean-style Soy Sauce

Enough for 2 salads
PREPARATION TIME: 15 minutes

2 tablespoons soy sauce
2 tablespoons salted anchovy
  extract, or Thai fish sauce
3 tablespoons green plum
  extract, or 1½ tablespoons
  sugar
1 tablespoon light corn syrup
1 tablespoon sesame oil
1 tablespoon grated garlic
2 tablespoons chili pepper
  powder

Combine all the ingredients in a bowl
and mix well.

Note This all-purpose sauce can be refrigerated for up to 2 weeks. Make it in quantity and keep it on hand to use as a sauce for stews and hot pots, as a salad dressing, and to season soups.

Salad with Soy-sauce Dressing

Serves 2

¼ head of loose leaf lettuce, cut into bite-sized pieces
10 perilla leaves, cut into bite-sized pieces
½ small cucumber, halved and sliced diagonally
3 tablespoons All-purpose Korean-style Soy Sauce (see above)
2 tablespoons rice vinegar

Mix all the vegetables together in a bowl. Combine the All-purpose Korean Style Soy Sauce and the vinegar to make the dressing and drizzle over the salad.

The All-purpose Korean-style Soy Sauce used with the Potato Pancakes in episode 3 of *Crash Landing on You*

📺 A group of housewives come to inspect the woman from the "south" who calls herself Jeong-hyeok's fiancée. The pancakes they bring as a gift are even more delicious when eaten with this Korean-style Soy Sauce.

Yangnyeom Fried Chicken

Serves 2

12 oz (350 g) readymade fried chicken pieces
Sweet and Salty Yangnyeom Sauce (see below)
1 tablespoon walnuts

1 Warm up the fried chicken in the microwave. Pour the Sweet and Salty Yangnyeom Sauce over it while the chicken is still hot, and mix evenly.

2 Chop the walnuts, and sprinkle over the chicken.

Sweet and Salty Yangnyeom Sauce

Serves 2

Enough for 2 servings of Yangnyeom Fried Chicken
PREPARATION TIME: 5 minutes

2 tablespoons gochujang paste
½ tablespoon soy sauce
1 tablespoon chili powder
2 tablespoons light corn syrup
1 tablespoon sugar
1 tablespoon water

Combine all the ingredients in a bowl and mix well to make the yangnyeom sauce.

Note Sweet and salty yangnyeom sauce is a seasoning that is used frequently to flavor meat and vegetables in Korean cooking. Sweet and salty fried chicken coated with yangnyeom sauce is a standard fast food in South Korea, and is very popular with kids as well as adults. It's great as an appetizer to eat with drinks.

The Yangnyeom Sauce Used in Episode 8 of *Start-Up*

In order to cheer up her friends who are feeling down because their work is not going well, Dal Mi gives them a feast of chicken served with sweet and salty yangnyeom sauce.

Everett Collection/アフロ

Shrimp with Gejang Sauce

Serves 4

20 fresh shrimp
3 garlic cloves
2 red chili peppers
Gejang Sauce (see below)

1 Remove the antennae from the shrimp. Peel and slice the garlic, and cut the chili pepper into thin rounds. Do not peel the shrimp—put them as is in a container, and put in enough chilled gejang sauce to cover them. Add the garlic and chili pepper and marinate the shrimp overnight in the refrigerator.

2 After marinating overnight, transfer the sauce, garlic and chili pepper to a pan and bring to a boil. Cool and chill the sauce completely, pour over the shrimp again and refrigerate. The shrimp are best to eat after two days.

Gejang Sauce

Enough for 20 shrimp
PREPARATION TIME: 20 minutes

¼ onion
1 dried shiitake mushroom
¼ apple
3 garlic cloves
1 piece ginger
⅔ cup (150 ml) soy sauce
1 tablespoon plus 2 teaspoons light soy sauce
6½ tablespoons mirin
3½ tablespoons green plum extract, or plum wine

1 tablespoon sugar
1½ cups (350 ml) water
2 pieces kombu seaweed, each 2-inch (5 cm) square
5 black peppercorns
3 red Thai chili peppers

1 Put all the ingredients into a large pot over high heat. When the pot comes to a boil lower the heat to medium, and simmer for 15 minutes.

2 Strain the liquid through a sieve. Refrigerate when it has cooled.

Note In South Korea this sauce is a traditional marinade for crab, but these days you'll find it used with abalone, sea snails or oysters too. Crab can be expensive, so here I've made the dish with shrimp, which is also delicious!

The Crab with Gejang Sauce in Episode 10 of *What's Wrong With Secretary Kim?*

In order to make Kim Mi So's older sisters accept that he is in a relationship with her, Young Joon wolfs down crab with gejang sauce at an all-you-can-eat crab restaurant. Mi So and her sisters observe this rather coolly.

Everett Collection/アフロ

Dadaegi Mixed Noodles

Serves 2

2 servings fresh Chinese egg noodles
2 servings Dadaegi Spicy Meat
  Sauce (see below)
2 tablespoons readymade sesame sauce
1 tablespoon rice vinegar
Fresh cilantro, for garnish

Cook the noodles following the packet instructions. Rinse under running water and drain well. Put the noodles in a bowl and mix in the Dadaegi Spicy Meat Sauce and sesame sauce. Sprinkle with the vinegar and serve garnished with the fresh cilantro.

Dadaegi Spicy Meat Sauce

4 servings
PREPARATION TIME: 20 minutes

1 tablespoon sesame oil
1 tablespoon vegetable oil
2 green onions, finely minced
3 oz (80 g) ground pork or beef
½ onion, minced

SEASONING MIX
1½ tablespoons chili powder
1 tablespoon grated garlic
1 tablespoon soy sauce
1 tablespoon light soy sauce
1 tablespoon sugar

1 Put the sesame and vegetable oils and minced green onion in a frying pan over low heat and stir-fry until fragrant

2 When the green onion is lightly browned, add the ground meat and stir-fry. Add the minced onion and continue stir-frying.

3 When the onion is translucent, add the Seasoning Mix ingredients and mix. Stir-fry over medium heat for about 5 minutes.

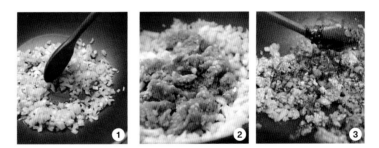

The Dadaegi Spicy Meat Sauce at Bar-Restaurant Danbam in *Itaewon Class*

This sauce is the seasoning base used for the Soft Tofu Stew on page 13, which appears in the episode when Danbam's soft tofu stew is the winning dish in the TV show *The Best Food Stall*. Viewers share Sae-ro-yi's happiness as he shouts out with joy.

ALBUM/アフロ

Egg Fried Rice

Serves 2
PREPARATION TIME: 20 minutes

¼ zucchini
¼ carrot
½ onion
4 slices canned luncheon meat
1 tablespoon vegetable oil
1½ cups (300 g) cooked rice
Simple Soy-sauce Dressing (below)
2 eggs
Pepper, to taste

1 Cut the zucchini, carrot, onion and luncheon meat into small dice. Heat a frying pan, put in the vegetable oil, put in the vegetables and luncheon meat and stir-fry.

2 When the onion is translucent clear a space in the middle of the frying pan. Put the rice and Simple Soy-sauce Dressing into the space, mix with the other ingredients and stir-fry.

3 Fry the eggs. Divide the rice between two plates and top each with a fried egg. Season with pepper to taste.

Simple Soy-sauce Dressing

Enough for 2 servings of Egg Fried Rice
PREPARATION TIME: 5 minutes

1 tablespoon soy sauce
1 tablespoon mirim or mirin
1 tablespoon perilla oil or sesame oil
1 teaspoon grated garlic

Just mix all the ingredients together well. It's very convenient to make this is in quantity and store it in the refrigerator!

Note Simply adding this sauce to boiled spinach or bean sprouts creates a delicious side dish.

The Egg Fried Rice in Episode 1 of *Itaewon Class*

On the morning before Sae-ro-yi starts at his new high school, he cooks egg fried rice for his father, a dish he makes very well. His father compliments Sae-ro-yi by telling him "You've gotten better." Sae-ro-yi answers him by saying "Like father, like son."

ALBUM/アフ

Chapter 6

Great When You Are Busy! Make-ahead Korean Dishes

Makes 20 quail eggs
PREPARATION TIME: 20 minutes

20 precooked canned or
  vacuum-packed quail eggs
1 dried shiitake mushroom
4 garlic cloves, peeled
10 shishito peppers or other
  mild green chili peppers

SEASONING MIX
¾ cup (200 ml) water
4 tablespoons soy sauce
4 tablespoons light corn syrup
1 tablespoon sugar

Simmered Quail Eggs Mechurial Jorim 메추리알조림

Everett Collection/アフロ

The Simmered Quail Eggs in Episode 15 of *It's Okay to Not Be Okay*

Moon Young loses her appetite because of the trauma she's been through. Joo Ri's mother makes her congee and simmered quail eggs. Moon Young is grateful for the kindness of others.

1 Put the Seasoning Mix ingredients in a pan and add the quail eggs, shiitake mushroom and garlic. Simmer over medium heat.

2 When the quail eggs have started to turn brown, add the shishito peppers and turn the heat down to low. Continue simmering until there is very little liquid left in the pan.

Note This is a nutritious dish that is easy to eat, so it's good for children too. It's also terrific as a drinking snack.

Serves 2
PREPARATION TIME: 10 minutes

**4 oz (110 g) shredded dried
  squid**
1½ tablespoons mayonnaise
1 teaspoon sesame oil
Sesame seeds, for garnish

SEASONING MIX
1 tablespoon gochujang paste
**½ tablespoon chili pepper
  powder**
1 tablespoon light corn syrup
1½ tablespoons water
1 teaspoon grated garlic
**1 teaspoon green plum extract,
  or 1 teaspoon sugar**

Dried Squid with Chili Jinmichaebokk-eum 진미채볶음

Everett Collection/アフロ

**The Numerous Dishes in
Episode 9 of *The King:
Eternal Monarch***

Prime Minister Koo eats the
savory snacks made by her
mother. Her mother tells her that
the customer who came to get his
umbrella looked just like Lee Lim.
Prime Minister Koo warns her it
would be the end if a rumor spread
that she had a son who was a rebel.

1 Cut the dried squid into 2 inch (5 cm)
pieces with scissors and put into a bowl.
Mix with the mayonnaise.

2 Put the Seasoning Mix ingredients into
a frying pan over medium heat. When
the mixture comes to a boil turn off the
heat, add the Step 1 ingredients and stir
to coat.

3 Stir in the sesame oil and sprinkle
with sesame seeds to finish.

Note This is put on top of plain rice and wrapped in flavored gim
or nori seaweed in South Korea. It's also great as a snack with beer!

Serves 2
PREPARATION TIME: 20 minutes

2 cups (200 g) soybean sprouts
1 teaspoon sesame oil
Sesame seeds, for garnish

SEASONING MIX
1 tablespoon chili pepper
** powder**
½ tablespoon light soy sauce
2 tablespoons minced green
** onions**
½ tablespoon grated garlic
½ tablespoon salt
1 teaspoon sugar

Korean-style Soybean Sprouts Kongnamul-muchim 콩나물무침

Everett Collection/アフロ

The Soybean Sprouts in Episode 16 of *Something in the Rain*

 Jin-Ah makes dinner instead of her mother. As the family eats rice, soup and soybean sprouts, her mother tells Jin-Ah that she must have an arranged meeting for a potential husband. The atmosphere around the table turns dark.

1 Rinse the soybean sprouts lightly.

2 Put the soybean sprouts in a pan of boiling water. Cover with a lid and boil for 4 minutes. Drain and rinse the soybean sprouts with cold water, then drain again.

3 Put the Seasoning Mix ingredients into a bowl.

4 Put the boiled soybean sprouts in another bowl and mix with the sesame oil. Add the ingredients from Step 3, and mix in with your hands, rubbing the bean sprouts.

5 Sprinkle with sesame seeds to finish.

Note Coating the boiled bean sprouts with sesame oil prevents them from getting watery and the flavors dissipating. The seasonings won't stick to the bean sprouts if you just stir with chopsticks or a fork, so rub them in gently with your hands.

Serves 2–4
PREPARATION TIME: 20 minutes

3 eggs
¼ carrot, minced
½ green onion, minced
1½ teaspoons salt
1 teaspoon grated garlic
1 teaspoon sesame oil
1 tablespoon vegetable oil
2 slices processed cheese

Korean Rolled Omelet Gyeran-mari 치즈계란말이

Everett Collection/アフロ

The Rolled Omelet in Episode 9 of *Mystic Pop-up Bar*

Kang Bae brings to the bar a woman who became separated from her son Joon-woo fifteen years ago. She is served the rolled cheese omelet that she says her son loved, as they start looking for him.

1 Break the eggs into a bowl. Add the minced carrot and green onion and mix.

2 Put in the salt, grated garlic and sesame oil and mix well.

3 Spread the vegetable oil into a frying pan and heat over medium heat. Pour in a third of the egg mixture. Cook while stirring until soft set, then top with the cheese slices and roll up to the far end of the pan.

3

4 Turn the heat down low. Add half the remaining egg mixture to the pan. When soft set, roll up to incorporate the existing roll. Repeat with the remaining egg mixture.

5 The omelet is done when it's lightly browned on the surface.

Note A square frying pan of the type used to make tamagoyaki (Japanese rolled omelet) works best for this recipe.

Serves 2–4
PREPARATION TIME: 25 minutes

**1 block firm tofu, about 12 oz
   (350 g)
2 tablespoons vegetable oil**

SEASONING MIX
**⅔ cup (150 ml) water
2 tablespoons chili pepper
   powder
2 tablespoons soy sauce
1 tablespoon salted shrimp
1 tablespoon green plum
   extract, or ½ tablespoon
   sugar
1 teaspoon grated garlic
1 tablespoon minced green
   onion**

Spicy Braised Tofu Dubu Jorim 두부조림

Everett Collection/アフロ

**The Dubu Jorim in Episode 3 of
Was It Love?**

Hye Jin invites Ha Nee's teacher Yeon Woo to the house and plies him with food. She throws a piece of spicy braised tofu in Ha Nee's mouth to stop her from asking her teacher strange questions.

1 Cut the tofu into ½ inch (1.5 cm) thick slices. Place on paper towels and leave to drain for about 10 minutes.

2 Combine all the Seasoning Mix ingredients in a bowl to make the sauce.

3 Heat a frying pan and add the vegetable oil. Pan-fry the tofu over medium heat.

4 When both sides are golden brown, add the sauce from Step 2 and simmer until the liquid in the pan is almost evaporated.

Note This is great with rice or drinks. Do make sure you use firm tofu for this, as it won't fall apart easily as it cooks. If you reduce the amount of chili powder by half, even people who don't like spicy food, or children, will like this.

Serves 2
PREPARATION TIME: 20 minutes

4 oz (110 g) small dried anchovies
3 tablespoons vegetable oil
2 tablespoons light corn syrup
1 tablespoon sesame oil
12 almonds, chopped
1 teaspoon roasted sesame seeds

SEASONING MIX

1 tablespoon green plum extract, mirim or mirin
2 tablespoons soy sauce
1 tablespoon sugar
1 teaspoon grated garlic
2 tablespoons water

Stir-fried Anchovies Myeolchi Bokkeum 멸치볶음

Everett Collection/77/7

The Stir-fried Anchovies in Episode 7 of *Start-Up*

Dal Mi invites Do San to her house, and has him meet her grandmother. Ji Pyung comes too, and the four of them sit at the table, while Do San, the grandmother and Ji Pyung desperately try to keep a secret from Dal Mi.

1 Put the dried anchovies in a frying pan and dry-roast them over low heat. Keep cooking them until they make a dry crackling sound in the pan and have dried out. Remove from the pan.

2 Combine all the Seasoning Mix ingredients in a bowl.

3 Put the combined Seasoning Mix ingredients in a heated frying pan. Bring to a boil, and put in the dried anchovies. Turn the heat down and simmer to reduce the sauce. When there is no liquid left in the pan, add the vegetable oil and stir-fry.

4 When the dried anchovies are coated with the sauce turn off the heat. Add the corn syrup, sesame oil, almonds and sesame seeds and mix.

5 Spread the anchovies out on a plate or tray to cool before serving.

Note Make sure to dry roast the dried anchovies well to get rid of their fishy smell. Once the sauce coats the dried anchovies they tend to stick together, so spread them out on a large plate for a while before transferring them to serving dishes.

Index of Recipes by Main Ingredient

Published by Tuttle Publishing, an imprint of
Periplus Editions (HK) Ltd.

www.tuttlepublishing.com

KANKOKU DRAMA NO TEIBAN GOHAN
Copyright © 2021 Hizesensei
English translation rights arranged with
TOKUMA SHOTEN PUBLISHING CO., LTD
through Japan UNI Agency, Inc., Tokyo

English translation by Makiko Itoh. English
translation copyright © 2022 Periplus Editions
(HK) Ltd.

Korean drama photographs pages 13, 15, 17, 19,
21, 23, 25, 27, 31, 45, 51, 61, 65, 71, 99, 113, 121,
courtesy of AFLO.

Photographs pages 6–8, 26, 30, 36, 42, 52, 60,
66, 94, 110, 112, 124, all Shutterstock.

ISBN 978-0-8048-5555-6

Distributed by

North America, Latin America & Europe
Tuttle Publishing
364 Innovation Drive
North Clarendon, VT 05759-9436 U.S.A.
Tel: 1 (802) 773-8930
Fax: 1 (802) 773-6993
info@tuttlepublishing.com
www.tuttlepublishing.com

Asia Pacific
Berkeley Books Pte. Ltd.
3 Kallang Sector #04-01
Singapore 349278
Tel: (65) 6741 2178
Fax: (65) 6741 2179
inquiries@periplus.com.sg
www.tuttlepublishing.com

26 25 24 23
10 9 8 7 6 5 4 3 2

Printed in China
2308EP

"Books to Span the East and West"

Tuttle Publishing was founded in 1832 in the small New England town of Rutland, Vermont [USA].
Our core values remain as strong today as they were then—to publish best-in-class books which bring
people together one page at a time. In 1948, we established a publishing outpost in Japan—and
Tuttle is now a leader in publishing English-language books about the arts, languages and cultures
of Asia. The world has become a much smaller place today and Asia's economic and cultural influence
has grown. Yet the need for meaningful dialogue and information about this diverse region has never
been greater. Over the past seven decades, Tuttle has published thousands of books on subjects
ranging from martial arts and paper crafts to language learning and literature—and our talented
authors, illustrators, designers and photographers have won many prestigious awards. We welcome
you to explore the wealth of information available on Asia at **www.tuttlepublishing.com**.